SAYING I DO TO YOUR CAREER

Dr. Raymond Holmes, GCDF

authorHOUSE®

AuthorHouse™
1663 Liberty Drive
Bloomington, IN 47403
www.authorhouse.com
Phone: 1 (800) 839-8640

Published by AuthorHouse 05/29/2015

ISBN: 978-1-4969-7446-4 (sc)
ISBN: 978-1-4969-7447-1 (e)

Library of Congress Control Number: 2015907743

Print information available on the last page.

Contents

List of Table

List of Figures

Acknowledgments

My first acknowledgment goes to my parents, the late Francis, and Abel Holmes. Without them, there would be no Dr. Raymond Holmes. They have been instrumental in getting me to where I am today. My second acknowledgment goes to my family (three sons) and fiancé, who put up with me through my educational journey.

Everyone has someone in their life they admire. Sometimes we may never tell the person or persons how much they inspired us. My role model is being revealed for the first time. He is the Distinguished Dr. Lenneal Henderson, from the University of Baltimore, where I completed my undergraduate degree in Business Administration.

Dr. Henderson is a walking encyclopedia. He is brilliant and very resourceful. I started branding myself to mirror him. He taught his students never stop learning, practice what you preach and learn something new every day. As the President of the Black Student Union and Vice President of the Student Government Association, Dr. Henderson was my mentor. Under his guidance, I was able to build the organization to one of the most vibrant student organizations on campus. I learned many things from Dr. Henderson concerning knowledge management and organizational leadership. He will always be an inspiration to me as I am to others.

I would like to express the deepest appreciation to Rose Young and the late Regina Smith, who created the concept of the "Workforce Doctor", a title that I held for over a decade. These ladies worked for Maryland's Department of Labor, Licensing and Regulations (DLLR). DLLR partnered with the Mayor's Office of Employment Development (MOED) in a One-Stop Career Center, where I worked, to provide employment and training assistance to job seekers.

One day, I began wearing a doctor's jacket with the title "Workforce Development Specialist" embroidered on it. This concept generated lots of attention. I have been featured in the Baltimore Sun, Center for Credentialing Education newsletter and referenced in other career development publications for my unorthodox strategies for helping job seekers.

Introduction

According to the U.S. Department of Education, over $112 billion dollars were invested in education in 2014 (Chantrill, C. 2014). Individuals attend higher educational institutions or vocational schools, which specialize in preparing individuals for a particular career path (i.e., healthcare, construction, education, and information technology). Through internships, on the job training and residency programs, individuals gain the hands-on experiences they need to demonstrate their ability to perform their profession.

While individuals spend countless hours mastering the skills, knowledge and abilities to compete in the labor market, they struggle with marketing their acquired skills to employers. One of the most difficult interview questions job candidates struggle to answer is "How has your education, and training prepared you for this job?" This question is challenging because job candidates have not mastered the concept of personal branding.

Moreover, many employers face the challenge of aligning an individual's skill sets and experiences to the needs of the organization. Recruiting the most qualified talent can be just as challenging because there are internal and external repercussions associated with hiring the right candidate. Studies have shown that poor hiring decisions cost at least $25,000 per person (Williams 2012, p. 1). Management personnel may also face challenges with aligning the qualifications of the job candidate to the branding of the organization, which may also have an effect on the turnover ratio in organizations.

Chapter 1

The Relationship Framework

We talk about the quality of product and service.
What about the quality of our relationships and the
quality of our communications and the quality of
our promises to each other? Max de Pree

To start an interviewing workshop, post the following question on chart paper on the wall: "What do you look for in a significant other?" On the other side of the room, post this question: "What do you look for in a career?" The responses for both of these questions are always interesting. The purpose of this exercise is to reveal to participants that the employment process is similar to dating or, as others may call it, courting. The term courting and dating will be used interchangeably throughout this publication. After about 10 minutes, I post my flip chart paper showing a general definition for both dating and interviewing.

One of the difficult challenges in both of these events revolves around one's confidence. Most people are hard on themselves. You are your worst critic. Therefore, instead of focusing on what could potentially go wrong, channel that energy and identify how you would benefit the party. Table 1 provides a side by side comparison of the definitions for a job interview and a date. Next, post these definitions once participants have pondered over how they distinguish the two.

Table 1. Dating vs. interviewing comparison

Dating	Interviewing
"Dating: Dating is a form of human courtship consisting of social activities done by two persons with the aim of each assessing the other's suitability as a partner in an intimate relationship or as a spouse. While the term has several senses, it usually refers to the act of meeting and engaging in some mutually agreed upon social activity in public, together, as a couple." (Brown, 2011).	"The interview is your opportunity to convince a potential employer that you are the best candidate for the job and that there is a strong "fit" between your skills and knowledge and those required for the position. You must be able to clearly articulate the skills you have to offer and describe how your past experiences demonstrate those skills. Completing a self-assessment as part of the career planning process will help you be able to clearly identify your skills, knowledge and areas of expertise" (Bookey, 2006).

Bookey (2006) and Brown (2011) share similar strategies for gaining confidence while on a date or job interview. These include a firm handshake, making eye contact, and smiling. Moreover, you might want to reminisce on similar situations where you did not possess the confidence, however you overcame the barrier and turned the situation into a positive event.

Chapter 1. Exercise Using the side by side comparison, identify how you define the attributes you look for in an employer and in a significant other.

	Employer	Significant other
What factors encouraged you to initiate the relationship?		
What attributes do you bring to the table?		
What stands out about you personality?		

Chapter 2

Management and Leadership Models

The greatest discovery of my generation is
that human beings can alter their lives by
altering their attitude of mind.
William James, Psychologist

Management involves the study of identifying strategies to make the organization and its human resources more productive. The Business Dictionary defines (2014) management as the organization and coordination of the activities of a business in order to achieve defined objectives. Management is often included as a factor of production along with machines, materials, and money (2014). Usually, when individuals work with processes and procedures, they fall in the management circle.

On the other hand, leadership theory involves the study of influencing and motivating employees to be productive. The Business Dictionary defines (2014) leadership as the individuals who are collectively regarded as the leaders in an organization. Leadership involves establishing clear visions, as well as coordinating and balancing the conflicting interests of internal and external stakeholders (Business Dictionary, 2014b).

Individuals who enjoy working around people and addressing human resource concerns would fall in the leadership circle. Discussing management and leadership theories and analysis in this publication will explain why employers and job candidates alike might focus their conversations in a particular direction. This section includes an overview of Maslow's Hierarchy of Needs, Motivational Factors, an organization's life cycle, Lewin's change theory, and S.W.O.T. analysis. There is an exercise included to demonstrate your understanding of the concepts.

Maslow's Hierarchy of Needs

Maslow's motivation theory contains five levels of basic human needs (Mudakavi, 2010). The theory is that people are motivated to achieve each level in order to reach the primary goal of self-actualization. However, often individuals may encounter many challenges along the way that prohibits them from fulfilling their objectives or levels of gratification. Individuals must start from the lowest hierarchical need before advancing to the next level, including physiological needs, safety, love and belonging, esteem, and self-actualization (Mosley, et. al, 2014).

Figure 1. Maslow's hierarchy of needs Diagram adapted from Royal Stock Photo.

Physiological needs

Maslow's theory is that our basic needs that must be addressed before any of the proceeding areas include air, food, and water (Goodman, 2013; Mosley, et. al, 2014). These elements fall under what Maslow calls the physiological needs. Without these elements, life would be impossible. According to Mudakavi (2010), the average person cannot live longer than five minutes without air. Food is important because it provides the body with the nutrients that make the body work, develop, and self-heal. Mudakavi (2010) also stated that the average person can survive from three to five days without water. Other factors including quality of air, water and food can impact the body's physiological functioning.

Organizations also have physiological needs. For organizations, these components include structure, capital, and customers. An organization without structure can suffer from management and leadership oversight. Capital is also another important attribute to the survival of an organization. If the funds are not flowing through an organization, it will be nearly impossible to keep the doors open. Finally, if the organizations do not have a customer base, it will not be able to generate the funding needed to function.

As a human's survival rate without its physiological needs may be determined by the body's weight and health conditions, an organization's survival rate may be determined based on its financial capital and market position. For example, a small business with little or no cash flow may have to declare bankruptcy within two years of its existence should a financial crisis emerge; this is because the financial structure may not be able to absorb the crisis (Pendrith, 2014). On the other hand, when one of Exxon's oil pipes erupted damaging many states' coastal lines, they lost a large percentage of customers (Ryan, 2014). Exxon was able to survive because of its financial capital. However, they still lost customers who may not have agreed with the handling of the crisis.

Safety needs

This second need, involving safety needs, can only ensue if one's physiological needs are achieved. Safety involves how secure and protected an individual feels (Asamoah et al., 2011; Mosley et. al, 2014). Some of these safety and security needs include health, financial, and personal security. As organizations are laying off thousands of employees because of the current economic conditions, no employee feels that their job is secure and protected.

Organizations also have safety needs. New competition can threaten the financial situation. Poor management and leadership can threaten the health of the organization as employees may opt to go elsewhere to work. Similar to job candidates' fear of job loss, many employers have not been able to maintain a qualified workforce.

Sense of belonging

The third component of the hierarchy involves an individual's feeling of being loved and being accepted by others. As human beings, we want to be loved and accepted by others (Goodman, 2013). This trait starts at a young age. A child may feel a sense of loneliness if they do not get the attention from their parents or if other children are teasing them. Job candidates may feel a sense of loneliness after not getting a job offer after countless interviews.

Organizations can also feel as if they are isolated. When the media publicizes a negative story regarding an organization, the organization can be affected. This isolation may be a result of investors, creditors, customers, and employees losing confidence in the organization. Minority businesses are often overlooked from obtaining government contracts because of their size and inability to compete with larger organizations (Bates & Bradford, 2006).

To address this situation and to build the confidence of small businesses, federal and state governments have initiated a solution to grow small businesses. Large organizations receiving government contracts to perform a job have to allocate a percentage of the contract to minority businesses because small businesses did not have the resources to compete for contracts (Bates & Bradford, 2006). Any private organizations who receive government contracts must also allocate a percentage of its contract to minority businesses (Lowrey, 2007). This initiative helped to increase minority businesses' sense of acceptance.

Self-esteem

Self-esteem deals with the way that individuals feel about themselves. Esteem often has to do with one's emotional assessment of themselves (Goodman, 2013; Asamoah et al., 2011). If an individual has low self-esteem, this can result in depression and a lack of the confidence needed to rebuild their esteem. For example, when people interview for jobs, their self-esteem is often low, and they are nervous because they lack the confidence that they could meet the employer's expectations.

Organizations have similar self-esteem issues. Many organizations do not have the confidence that they can attract the right people to work for them. Or, they may not be confident that they can get creditors to support them. When Wal-Mart started opening stores in many areas, they were forcing smaller businesses to close because they could not compete. While Wal-Mart's confidence and self-esteem were high, the opposite ensued for the smaller businesses.

Self-actualization

The final stage in the hierarchy of needs deals with how the individual sees himself and the contribution they can make. Maslow describes this level as the desire to accomplish everything that a person ever wanted to achieve (Asamoah, 2011). Considering this, personal branding comes to mind while discussing self-actualization. At this point, an individual has developed their identity, personality, and characteristics.

Some examples include a person determining that they want to be a singer, painter, CEO, or school teacher. At this stage in life, most people have either entertained or determined what type of work they want to explore. They may not have determined their career path though. Maslow believed that to understand this level of need, a person must not only achieve the previous needs but master them (Asamoah, 2011).

Many people may often go to college to study a particular discipline based on what they perceive their desired career to be. Half way through a major, they may change their career path. This process may never subside for many people. An unclear career path presents many challenges when asked by employer's questions such as "Why do you want to work here?" or "Why do you want to work in this industry?"

Studies had shown that it often takes organizations years after being in existence before they determine what is their market position or niche. Small business owners struggle with identifying their products or services (Pendrith, 2014). Often the reason for most business failures is that they have not fully developed its brand (Pendrith, 2014). Job candidates and organizations alike face challenges of finalizing who they are and what is their purpose for existing.

Chapter 2a. Exercise Identify your personal needs against your employment needs based on Maslow's hierarchy of needs theory

	Personal needs	Employment needs
Physiological needs		
Safety needs		
Sense of belonging		
Self-esteem		
Self-actualization		

Organizational Life Cycle

Organizations, like people, have similar characteristics. Understanding the organization's life cycle will give job seekers and hiring managers a better understanding of how to identify that a good fit exists between the two parties. Here, we personify an organization to illustrate the similarities between job candidates. Employers may ask job candidates the following questions during a job interview:

- What do you know about our organization?
- What articles have you read about our organization?

The purpose of these questions is to examine the job candidate's knowledge about the internal and external culture. This question is also to determine if the candidate obtained enough information to conclude they are a good fit for the organization's culture. Monroe (2013) stated,

> Most organizations want people who "fit in" and who "stand out." They want people who fit the culture and who excel in their work. In some organizations, in fact, culture fit is more important than skill, because there's a belief that skills often are more easily taught than the elusive "cultural fit (33)."

An organization's life cycle consists of four stages. These stages include birth, growth, maturity, and decline (International, 2013). You may often see management theorists add a fifth stage, which is death. To illustrate the components of the life cycle, two well-known computer manufacturing giants, Apple and Microsoft, are used to explain the phases of the life cycle. In addition to understanding the structure of an organization, it is equally important to understand the leadership vision. Using these two companies is not only good for explaining to job seekers the importance of researching the organization, but for observing the differences in leadership direction each of these entrepreneurs saw the business concept going.

Birth

The birth stage of an organization starts with an idea or concept of business. Some publications may refer to this stage as the "start-up" stage. Once an individual forms a business concept and executes an idea for the purpose of generating profits, the birth stage starts. Establishing a purpose for your business existence, and developing a plan of execution is essential to launching a business. According to an article published in Dun & Bradstreet, 33% of all start-up businesses fail within their first six months because they did not have a business plan (Pendrith, 2014).

The concept of Apple and Microsoft computers was born in 1976 out of a garage by Steve Jobs and Bill Gates (Manes & Andrews, 1983). The business concept started as a hobby, which ultimately created an "ah hah" moment for these guys. Both entrepreneurs were innovative and had a desire to start a business. However, Gates' and Jobs' vision on the direction they wanted to take the business differed (Sieczkowski, 2011). They both set out to individualize their strategies in the direction they wanted to take their business concepts.

From a job seeker's perspective, the birth of an individual's vision for their dream career may emerge at an early age based on family career history, educational institutions, and other entities and activities. Most children have been asked, "What do you want to be when you grow up?" This is a challenging question for children because they have not found their niche, nor have they gone through the self-identity phase where their personality, character, and other attributes were established. It is plausible to conclude that not establishing one's brand could be the reason individuals may be committed to taking any job until they have identified what career they actually want to pursue. If you have ever been around people who job hop, that is likely the reason.

Growth

During the growth stage (also known as the youth stage), organizations are looking to brand themselves and to create a targeted market for their products and services. Essentially, the growth stage is where the product or service starts to formulate or grow (Luxinnovation, 2008). A large investment of time and money, usually, takes place during this stage. Pendrith (2014) stated that 50% of businesses fail within the first two years because they first, fail to measure goals and objectives, and finally, have no means of differentiation from their competition. Organizations and job seekers alike must have a clear mission and vision established to guide their aspirations.

According to Manes and Andrews (1983), Jobs' vision was Apple Computers would dominate the computer business industry, while his counterpart, Gates, would operate the software side of the business. This plan would have established Jobs as the CEO of the company while Gates would only be managing a division of Apple. While Gates' created the Disc Operating System (DOS) application, under Jobs' vision, the operating system would be owned by Apple as well. Often, when an employer asks the question, "What do you know about our company?" They may be seeking to discover if you understand the dynamics of the business.

Gates, on the other hand, had other aspirations for his DOS system. Gates envisioned the DOS operating system would become obsolete under Jobs' proposal. Therefore, he branched off and created Microsoft as a standalone software company. The bottom-line here is that both Jobs and Gates sought out to create their brand and to corner the computing industry (branding will be discussed in a later chapter), and to grow the business.

Understanding the growth stage dynamics (not necessarily this complex) should help job candidates to answer the following interview question, "What stands out about you?" During this stage of an individual's career exploration, the job candidate may have narrowed down what profession they want to enter and begun to make investments in education and skill enhancements to compete in the industry. As previously mentioned, not differencing yourself from your competition does not yield good results. Employers are irritated when they hear the same default answer to that question, a default answer like, "I'm a hard worker" or "I'm dependable, honest etc." Job candidates need to be more creative during the growth stage of their career and to be able to articulate why they would make a difference in the profession as they seek to mature.

Maturity

During the maturity stage (also called the midlife stage), an organization seeks to develop plans to maintain the customer base while increasing its market share. The primary purpose of this stage is to focus on those internal and external factors, which may prohibit the organization from maturing. Pendrith (2014) also identified several dilemmas, which resulted in organizations failing within the first two years of existence including underestimating the competition, and poor marketing strategies to attract new customers. The unique challenge for Gates and Jobs here was that they were competing against one another.

Under the directions of Jobs, Apple Computers has revolutionized the computer world with its new innovative products from computers to iPads, and iPods. Apple stocks are high, as well as their consumer interest. Based on Apple's market share and customer base this organization has reached maturity. Mallin et al. (2011) stated that since Apple's introduction in 1984, the Mac computer has undergone many transformations but has always been known for its stylish design, high-performance levels, and competitive price. Today's version of the iMac desktop computer is targeted at educational and business customers.

On the other hand, Microsoft has also reached maturity with its breakthrough hardware, and software technology including Windows, tablets, MS Office Suite, and the X-Box. Another indication that Microsoft has reached maturity was its expansion to 12 markets in Europe, the Middle East, and Africa, and it has broadened its developer partner ecosystem to support those additional markets with local, relevant content (Anonymous, 2009). Likewise, job candidates and employees alike must put the pieces in place to not only get a job but to keep a job.

Once an employee or job candidate realizes their maturity point, they can make themselves more attractive to a potential employer. This maturity would be evident by the way you market your abilities and how the organization would benefit from hiring you. Since organizations are result driven, by demonstrating you're confident in not only marketing your skills, knowledge, and ability but delivering the expected outcomes, you reveal to an employer that you have matured within the job. Maturity for a job candidate would include explaining how the amount of education, experience, and track record of success yield the desired results the organization is seeking.

Decline

During the declining stage, organizations begin to experience setbacks in several areas including sales, customers, and market visibility. Gupta (2010) stated that an organization enters the declining phase when it experiences continuous reduction in resources and revenue over a substantial period. Several factors may contribute to an organization's decline including laws, competition, and profit share (Gupta, 2010; Pendrith, 2014).

Apple experienced a short period of decline in profits after the launch of the iPhone. While the iPhone sales generated over $33 million in sales, Apple's profits fell for the first time in 11 years (Hussan, 2013). This decline was a result of the costs it took to manufacture the new iPads and Macbooks, and the fact that prices weren't boosted accordingly (Hussan, 2013). Because Apple had capital on hand to offset the profit loss, the organization was not impacted.

A 2013 article published in Forbes magazine suggested that Microsoft profits were declining because of lower PC sales and the company not performing well in the mobile sector (Arora, 2013). However, despite the declining sales to those sectors, Microsoft's consumer and device revenues grew (Arora, 2013). This decline was only temporary for Microsoft because they have other resources to shift around to prevent moving into the death phase of the life cycle.

Organizations may decline when they fail to remain competitive with their competitors (Pendrith, 2014). This decline can result from internal and external situations. An example of an external decline would be Pepsi advertising a sale on its products, let's say, buy two cases of Pepsi and get a third case for free. You can be assured that Coca Cola will follow with its own sale to counter Pepsi's sale. Failing to do so will result in a loss of profit for Coke products as even loyal customers of Coke may take advantage of Pepsi's offer. Several dynamics come into play here as Coke's customer may find a Pepsi product that they are satisfied with and might not return to Coke. This dynamic can work both ways.

As discussed earlier, a marriage is formed between an organization and job candidate once they both engage in the hiring agreement. Therefore, if organizations do not provide up-to-date training for its members, they may experience a decline in productivity and a lack of motivation from staff. Job candidates that do not update their knowledge and skill sets for their career occupations lessen their chances for a promotion or maintaining a competitive edge for future employment opportunities. This will ultimately result in possible death of the employer-employee relationship.

Death

Usually when an organization is near the death stage of the life cycle, it needs to be placed on life support. This period calls for the intervention of organizational change agents to identify and address the issues before the organization collapses. Gupta (2010) identified five critical phases of an organization that are within the death stage:

- Blinded stage
- Inaction stage
- Faulty stage
- Crises stage
- Dissolution stage.

The blinded stage occurs when leadership fails to recognize that problems exist within the organization (Gupta, 2010). The inaction stage results when management does have evidence that problems do exist, but does not act to address the issue (Gupta, 2010). The faulty stage emerges when management knows that they are under a lot of pressure from internal and external stakeholders to address the issues (Gupta, 2010). Conflicts transpire when tough decisions must be made to revive the organization (Gupta, 2010). Finally, once the dissolution stage occurs, it is a sign that management has done everything that it could have done to revive the organization, and all efforts have failed (Gupta, 2010).

Both Apple and Microsoft appear to be in good health and are aware of their internal and external surroundings. On the other hand, Eastern Airlines was one of the largest airline contenders from 1926 to 1991. However, Eastern started its decline in the 1980s due to disputes with labor unions (Barlett, 2010). Despite management's efforts to revive itself, the airline bankrupted in 1991(Barlett, 2010). Eastern's death was a result of internal conflicts, and could not be addressed.

Equivalently, marriages and employment relationships also go through the death stage once one or both parties come to the conclusion that they have used many strategies to correct the concerns with no positive outcomes. Believe it or not, job candidates may experience each of the five life cycle stages during the job interview. The interview may start out great; the candidate is marketing himself and explaining how his expertise would benefit the organization. All of a sudden, here comes the bombshell: the employer asks the candidate to reveal something about themselves or the candidate may have to explain why they were terminated from a previous job.

Chapter 2b. Exercise This project is twofold. Using the life cycle grid, first, name a project that you initiated on the job and that the final outcome was not successful. Finally, identify a project that you initiated and that the final outcome was successful. Identify at which stage did you start to see a change in the project?

	Birth	Growth	Maturity	Decline	Death
Failed project					
Good project					

Lewin's Change Theory

Kurt Lewin is a psychologist who in the 20th Century identified three phases which individuals or organizations need to reduce resistance to changes in the environment (Cummings & Vortey, 2014). Lewin's theory holds that while some people come ready to change, others take longer to let go of their comfort zone. Managing change in an organization can be challenging if the leadership cannot identify those internal and external concerns, which may result in a change in behavior or productivity. Figure 2 displays an image of how the change process takes place

Figure 2. Ice Cube depicting the change process.
adapted from Royal Stock Photo.

For example, managers must address such issues as working with a diverse workforce or the economy forcing a reduction of hours. Organizations would like to have a formal culture where the entire workforce's ethics, performance, and personality fit its vision and values. However, because some organizational members' values and beliefs differ from the organization's view, informal organization cliques are formed resulting in a conflict between cultures. Lewin identifies three phases, which serve as a strategy for promoting change in the organization or individual. These include unfreezing current conditions, transitioning behavior, and freezing the new conditions.

Unfreezing

Unfreezing the current conditions of an organization can be the most challenging because either party, including internal and external entities, may not be willing to compromise their beliefs or positions. Cummings and Vortey (2014) contended that the unfreezing phase involves reducing those forces maintaining the organization's behavior at its present level. This process is the toughest because it involves letting go of your current beliefs and putting all of your cards on the table with the other parties involved and working through your differences (Cummings & Vortey, 2014).

For example, despite studies revealing that going outside of the organization to hire someone with a fresh perspective and new ideas is beneficial, many managers still elect to promote from within. Change in this situation will not occur until management is open to explore other possibilities for achieving organizational goals. A job candidate that believes that his one resume will fit all job opportunity requirements and elects not to customize his resume for each job is not willing to change his behavior.

Transition

The period of transitioning can begin once all parties have agreed to put aside their differences and come to the table with an open mind. This process is also difficult in the change model because individuals may have to compromise and give-up something they cherish in order to find common ground for all members. Cummings and Vortey (2014) stated that this step shifts the behavior of the organization, department, or individual to a new level, which involves intervening in the system to develop new behaviors, values, and attitudes through changes in the organizational structures and processes.

After the management team who will only promote from within the organization and the job candidate who will not customize his resume have agreed to move toward considering other strategies and resolutions, the transitioning phase is underway. Unions are often trapped in this phase where all parties are at the table trying to convince one another that their process is best. Many times change agents, or conflict resolution specialists are hired to facilitate these sessions, especially when values and beliefs are at stake.

Refreezing

After the debates have subsided and the parties have agreed to a solution to the situation or event, the refreezing phase begins. Because we do not live in a utopian society, this process can be ongoing. Cummings and Vortey (2014) describe this phase as stabilizing the organization at a new state of equilibrium through supporting mechanisms that reinforce the new organizational state. In other words, a consensus is made by the parties involved to change, or at least to attempt to abase the change before denouncing it. If the initiative does not work, then the parties will return to the table with new recommendations.

Let's review the management team and the job candidate who are against any efforts of change. Assume that these parties have agreed to let go of their current ways of doing business and put aside their values and beliefs and are open for suggestions and recommendations. The manager is being presented with data and other information revealing the benefits of hiring external personnel. The management team may also have supporting data to support his decision. Likewise, the job candidate is presented with information from hiring managers on hiring practices. These entities have agreed to incorporate some recommendations.

Under the new mindsets of each party, change begins to take place as management expands its hiring practices and the job candidate customizes his resume based on the wants and needs of the employer. If management or the job candidate finds success with the implementation of these changes, then the change process was effective. However, if the change efforts have failed, then the process starts over at step 1.

Chapter 2. Exercise Using the three phases of the change model, identify and explain a situation or event where you resisted change, and where you succeeded at the change process with another individual or group.

	Resisted change	Promoted change
Describe the situation requiring a change		
Identify the methods or strategies used to neutralize yourself or party's values and beliefs to participate in the change process		
What compromises were agreed upon as the new change took effect?		

SWOT Analysis

A SWOT analysis is used to identify the strengths, weakness, opportunities and threats of a project or an organization (Beverly, 2010). Couples who attend marriage counseling use a similar analysis, such as a SWOT, to help them determine if they are compatible. If used correctly, a SWOT analysis can help to save time and money.

Strengths

Addams et al. (2013) defined strengths as the skills, education, experience, networking, character traits, and other attributes that one has that help to distinguish them from others. The problem with most managers or job candidates is their inability to market their strengths. When employers ask "Tell me something about yourself?" or "What standout about you?", job candidates should focus on their strengths. Attributes such as "hard worker" or "dependable" are not strengths.

Managers struggle with marketing the strengths of the organization to potential candidates to convince them that their organization would be a better choice for work. For example, an organization might discuss why their benefit package is better than its competitors. A job candidate might discuss their successes, such as increased sales and profits, or the implementation of a successful training and development program that would benefit the employer's needs. As we will discuss in the Problem/ Solution section, job candidates must understand the employer's needs before certifying himself as a good match for the job.

Weaknesses

Weaknesses are defined as one's gap in skills, knowledge, abilities, networking, character traits, and other attributes (Addams, 2013). Every attribute that an individual may define as a weakness may not necessarily be a weakness depending on the environment or culture one is entering. For example, micro-managing may be considered a weakness because no employee wants to be followed all of the time, as if they are in a prison. However, this trait may be a strength for individuals who are in a training and development role, because often corrective actions measures may need to be employed.

However, a true weakness may be an employer's inability to reduce their turnover ratio, or a job candidate who is entering into a culture where a large percentage of its environment is bilingual. Having weaknesses is not a crime. Individuals often cringe when they are asked, "What are your weaknesses?" The key to answering that question is to understand the culture you are applying to work in. For example, if you know that you are not bilingual, when seeking a position in an organization where over 50% of the staff is bilingual, to address this weakness, you might want to explain how you are going to take a course to improve your skills. The problem is not having a weakness; it is what you are doing to address the weakness.

According to Goodrich (2013) strengths and weaknesses are considered internal factors. Internal factors consist of those resources and experiences that are available to the organization. These include:

- Financial resources, such as funding, sources of income and investment opportunities
- Physical resources, such as your company's location, facilities and equipment

- Human resources, such as employees, volunteers and target audiences
- Current processes, such as employee programs, department hierarchies and software systems

Similarly, job candidates have internal factors of their own. Marketing the hosts of skills, knowledge, and abilities are equally important. One might want to discuss such factors like education, affiliations, recognitions and accomplishments. It would not also hurt to discuss some challenges you faced and explain your course of action for addressing the challenge.

Opportunities

Many organizations and people alike have taken advantage of many opportunities to address a weakness or to enhance one's strengths. Addams (2013) identified many areas in which organizations and people may seek to find opportunities. These include technology, legislation, social values, economy, demographics of population, and geographical conditions.

Organizations and individuals may choose areas in which to seek opportunities based on the types of products and services of an organization. For example, an organization that is regulated by many rules and regulations might seek opportunities within the legislation area. Moreover, if an individual seeking to improve their computer skills may seek opportunities within the technology area.

An employee evaluation is a good example of an assessment tool, which allows for an employee to be assessed in order to identify his strengths, weaknesses, and areas for improvement (or opportunities). Let's say that the manager expresses to the employee that he needs to work on his time management skills. Rather than taking the recommendation as a negative criticism, the employee should use this situation as an opportunity to identify strategies or workshops to help him improve this deficiency. Likewise, organization leaders should also use this situation or similar events as an opportunity to implement strategies to address situations in the future to demonstrate that they invest in their human resources.

Threats

Threats are viewed as those situations or events, which may prohibit or present challenges for an individual or organization to perform. As for opportunities of threat, Addams (2013) also identified technology, legislation, social values, economy, demographics of population, and geographical conditions. An example of a threat for a job candidate would be competing with individuals who might have more education and experience. This threat can fall within a number of those areas because the economic conditions might prohibit one from obtaining more education, or an employer, as presented above, may need to hire someone who is bilingual to meet the need of the population whey serve.

In hindsight, possessing less education and experience may be threats to an individual's ability to be hired because employers would generally hire the candidate with the best qualifications. A threat for an employer could be other employers who are able to pay its employees more or offer a better benefit package. The threat results from potentially losing good employees who might be motivated by the money and might want to abandon ship.

Organizations and individuals must continuously scan the environment for potential threats and orchestrate plans to counter that threat. Goodrich (2013) identified the opportunities and threats of an organization as external factors. These factors, as identified by Goodrich, consist of those components that the organization does not have control over including:

- Market trends, such as new products and technology or shifts in audience needs
- Economic trends, such as local, national and international financial trends
- Funding, such as donations, legislature and other foundations
- Demographics, such as a target audience's age, race, gender and culture

Job candidates also experience external factors that may interfere with landing a career. Rising tuition cost or changes in education requirements may prohibit one from finishing a degree program to become employable. For example, to become a certified public accountant, individuals can no longer sit for the CPA test with only a bachelor's degree. Students are now required to obtain 150 credit hours to qualify to take the CPA exam (AICPA, 2014). Keeping abreast of such internal and external factors based on a S.W.O.T. analysis would help to provide an assessment of an organization and job candidate.

Chapter 2. Exercise Identify your strengths, weaknesses, opportunities, and threats, and explain what you plan to do to turn these attributes into strengths.

Attributes	Your attributes	Corrective action
Strengths		
Weaknesses		
Opportunities		
Threats		

Chapter 3

Employment Laws

No man is above the law and no man is below it;
nor do we ask any man's permission when we ask him to obey it.
Obedience to the law is demanded as a right; not asked as a favor.
Theodore Roosevelt

With more and more people leaving the workforce, the baby boomer era is rapidly becoming a thing of the past. Therefore, the workforce is more diverse than ever before. Workforce diversity (also called cultural diversity) exists when there is a difference in race, ethnicity, gender, disability, age, sexual orientation, religion, and other aspects of culture (Pope, 2012). Over the last decade, we have seen a major shift in the workplace, such as marriage equality, a rise of individuals with disabilities entering the workforce, as well as an increase in immigrants' entering the workforce (Pope, 2012).

As workplace dynamics have shifted over the last two decades, it is plausible to conclude that the interpretations of employment laws have also shifted. This shift in workplace dynamics has resulted in the differences in interpretation between the older and younger generations. This generational gap has resulted in the unofficial changes to the components of Title VII of the Civil Rights Act.

For example, traffic light signals are interpreted the same worldwide. Red means stop, yellow means slow down so that the driver will not potentially run the red light, and the green light means go. However, it appears that in today's society the unofficial rule for a yellow light means that the driver can speed up to make it through the light before it turns red. Below are the original definitions of the components of Title VII and today's interpretation of those laws.

Civil Rights Act

Title VII of the Civil Rights Act of 1964 was created to protect job candidates and employees from being discriminated against in the workplace (CSOSA, 2013). Title VII protected employees from employment discrimination based upon the job candidates' or employees' race, religion, sex, national origin, disabilities, age, and equal pay (CSOSA, 2013).

A central component in Title VII is to protect job candidates from illegal hiring practices, and employees from promotional opportunities on the job (CSOSA, 2013). The following components of the Civil Rights Employment laws and its definitions are as follows:

> The U.S. Equal Employment Opportunity Commission (EEOC) is responsible for enforcing federal laws that make it illegal to discriminate against a job applicant or an employee (CSOSA, 2013; U.S. EEOC, (2013). The EEOC provides protection with regards to race, color, religion, sex, national origin, age, or disability discrimination (U.S. EEOC, 2013). U.S. EEOC (2013) also stated that It is also illegal to discriminate against a person because the person complained about discrimination, filed a charge of discrimination, or participated in an employment discrimination investigation or lawsuit.

Age discrimination

Under Title VII of the Civil Rights Act, Employers cannot refuse to hire individuals based on age, pay lower wages, or segregate such employees from the workforce (CSOSA, 2013; Lemov, 2014). CSOSA (2013) stated:

> The Age Discrimination in Employment Act of 1967 (ADEA) protects individuals who are 40 years of age or older from employment discrimination based on age. The ADEA's protections apply to both employees and job applicants. Under the ADEA, it is unlawful to discriminate against a person because of his/her age with respect to any term, condition, or privilege of employment, including hiring, firing, promotion, layoff, compensation, benefits, job assignments, and training.

According to an article published in Forbes, a 54-year-old woman won a \$193,236 lawsuit in 2008 against her company because she was fired, despite scoring high on all evaluations (Lemov, 2014). While age discriminations cases can be hard to prove, what was stunning about this case were the comments her employer made about Debra Moreno to staff. The employer was reported as saying "she looked like a bag of bones" and "sounds old on the telephone" (Lemov, 2014).

The age gap in the workplace has significantly widened. The argument on age discrimination in the past focused primarily on individuals' over the age threshold and their ability to achieve organizational goals in a timely manner (Calo et al., 2013). Therefore, speed might have been the reasons for denying employment opportunities and promotional opportunities to people over 40 years-old.

Many employers that have an older management structure in place often want to hire older staff. The same practices apply in the reverse for organizations with a younger management structure in place. The perception is that there may not be much deviation concerning culture fit or communication and values. The older staff contends that the younger staff is not respectful, while the younger staff insists that the older staff do not want to try anything new.

What is most interesting about this culture clash and should result in further studies is the war over ethics. The manner of each party results in many business practice conflicts. The older group argues that the younger group would cut corners and engage in unethical business practices in order to stay afloat. On the other hand, the younger group argues that the older group is too accommodating to customers, even if it is apparent that the customer is at fault. The generational gap considering those dynamics has resulted in a shift of interpretations over the original age discrimination law.

American with Disabilities Act

Under Title VII of the Civil Rights Act, employers cannot refuse to hire individuals because of a disability. CSOSA (2012) defined the Americans with Disabilities Act of 1990 (ADA) as prohibiting discrimination against qualified individuals with disabilities in job application procedures, such as hiring, firing, advancement, compensation, job training, and other terms, conditions, and privileges of employment. Further, employers must provide reasonable accommodations to such individuals.

Traditional disabilities discrimination claims focused more on physical and mental capacity to do the job. Today, the focus of ADA has shifted to healthcare expenses for the employer. It is plausible that employers make hiring or promotional decisions not only based on qualifications, but healthcare expenses were also a factor as revealed in many ADA lawsuits.

In 2012, the U.S. District Court filed an ADA lawsuit against Baltimore County government (Knezevich, 2012). A former highway worker was forced to retire after learning that he had a pacemaker surgery in 2010 (Knezevich, 2012). The employee, William Galanti, was cleared by his doctor to return to work. However, a doctor, hired by the county, revealed Galanti's medical records found him not fit to return to work (Knezevich, 2012). The lawsuit was filed after Galanti was harassed by his employer on when he was going to retire. This case was settled for $500,000.

Many employment applications ask a job candidate if they have any pending worker compensation cases, while other questions ask would you need reasonable accommodations for the job. These questions are designed to eliminate potential financial risks and liabilities to the employer. This behavior makes the ADA compliance more about costs verses disabilities.

Gender discrimination

Under Title VII of the Civil Rights Act, employers are prohibited from denying employment or treating individuals differently based on sexual orientation or gender. CSOSA (2013) defines gender discrimination, also known as sex-based discrimination:

> It is unlawful to discriminate against any employee or applicant for employment because of his/her sex in regard to hiring, termination, promotion, compensation, job training, or any other term, condition, or privilege of employment. Title VII also prohibits employment decisions based on stereotypes and assumptions about abilities, traits, or the performance of individuals on the basis of sex. Title VII prohibits both intentional discrimination

and neutral job policies that disproportionately exclude individuals on the basis of sex and that are not job related.

About two decades ago, gender discrimination primarily involved women being treated unfairly in the workplace or during the employment process. Discrimination against women has taken a back seat to the issues involving gays and lesbians in the workplace. Today, the interpretation of the gender/sex discrimination law appears to be focused on gays and lesbians' rights in the workplace. Gay and lesbian rights advocates have become a dynamic force in protecting the rights of this protected class in the workforce and abroad.

A recent study revealed that workplace discrimination is a persistent problem for many lesbian, gay, bisexual and transgender individuals (LGBT) (McCabe, 2014). According to a 2013 survey published by the Pew Research Center, at least 20% of LGBT workers stated that they have been discriminated or treated unfairly by an employer (McCabe, 2014). Moreover, 90% of transgender people said they have been harassed on the job, while 26% stated that they have been terminated because of their gender identity. Despite these stunning results Kevin Cramer, a congressional representative, insists that LGBT workplace discrimination does not exists.

The lesson here is that employers and job candidates alike, despite personal beliefs, must learn to embrace the changing dynamics in the workplace. Everyone bears some differences in one way or another, which may spark some attention. However, the goal here is to respect one another and, if at all possible, learn about different cultures other than your own.

National origin discrimination

Under Title VII of the Civil Rights Act, treating people differently because they are from another country or part of the world is prohibited in employment (National origin is defined as individuals from a particular country) (CSOSA, 2012). The U.S. EEOC (2013) has stated:

> It is unlawful to harass a person because of his or her national origin. Harassment can include, for example, offensive or derogatory remarks about a person's national

origin, accent or ethnicity. Although the law doesn't prohibit simple teasing, offhand comments, or isolated incidents that are not very serious, harassment is illegal when it is so frequent or severe that it creates a hostile or offensive work environment or when it results in an adverse employment decision (such as the victim being fired or demoted) (U.S. EEOC, 2013).

Over the last 20 years, there has been an influx of individuals from different nationalities entering the U.S. workforce. This law forbids discrimination against individuals from any different nationality when it comes to any aspect of employment, including hiring, firing, pay, job assignments, promotions, layoff, training, fringe benefits, and any other term or condition of employment (U.S. EEOC, 2013), though interpretation of this law has shifted primarily to the Hispanic population.

It is no secret that for decades immigrants have been crossing the borders of the United States in search of a better future. The feuds over unauthorized immigrants in the workforce are alleged to be taking jobs from Americans. An unauthorized immigrant is:

> The unauthorized resident immigrant population is defined as all foreign-born non-citizens who are not legal residents. Most unauthorized residents either entered the United States without inspection or were admitted temporarily and stayed past the date they were required to leave. Unauthorized immigrants applying for adjustment to lawful permanent resident (LPR) status under the Immigration and Nationality Act (INA) Section 245(i) are unauthorized until they have been granted LPR status, even though they may have been authorized to work (Hoefer et al., 2010).

One of the major debates concerning the Hispanic population and the controversy over national origin is that Hispanics are taking jobs away from Americans. According to a 2013 study, 64% of Americans believe that immigrants coming to this country today mostly take jobs that Americans don't want (Jones et al., 2013). The same study also revealed that 56% of Americans believe that illegal immigrants hurt the economy by driving down wages for many Americans (Jones et al., 2013).

Race discrimination

Under Title VII of the Civil Rights Act, employers are prohibited from denying employment or treating individuals of a certain race differently because of race, color, or creed. According to CSOSA (2012), It is unlawful to discriminate against any employee or applicant for employment because of his/her race or color in regard to hiring, termination, promotion, compensation, job training, or any other term, condition, or privilege of employment. Title VII also prohibits employment decisions based on stereotypes and assumptions about abilities, traits, or the performance of individuals of certain racial groups. Title VII prohibits both intentional discrimination and neutral job policies that disproportionately exclude minorities and that are not job related.

In 2013, the EEOC filed a lawsuit against Battaglia Distributing Co. for racial discrimination (U.S. EEOC (2), 2013). The lawsuit alleged that racial slurs were used by both black and white supervisors to scold black employees. Management created a hostile work environment by allowing black hourly workers to be treated unfairly (U.S. EEOC (2) (2013). Despite the company dismissing the slurs as just "locker room talk," the EEOC did not buy the argument, citing that it was a clear violation of the Civil Rights Act (U.S. EEOC (2) (2013).

African Americans still continue to experience a high rate of racial discrimination in employment related matters. However, it is plausible that the controversy over illegal immigrants, primarily Hispanics, in the workforce allegedly taking jobs from American workers draw just as much attention. I have facilitated several workshops and met with employers who have expressed their personal opinions concerning the racial disparities against Hispanics in the workplace.

Many employers have stated that though a Hispanic individual is cleared by the government to legally work in the U.S., employers still feel that they are chastised by Americans for hiring Hispanics just to save money on salaries. This debate has all of the characteristics and racial dynamics that African Americans received while entering the workforce. This is history repeating itself. However, civil rights laws have been enhanced over the last two decades to further narrow the racial discrimination situations, and organizational leaders, job candidates, and employees have access to more resources and diversity training opportunities to combat such behavior.

Religious discrimination

Under Title VII of the Civil Rights Act, employers are prohibited from denying employment or treating individuals of a certain religion or faith differently. Further, it is also unlawful for employers to discriminate against individuals because of their religion in hiring, firing, and other terms and conditions of employment (CSOSA, 2012; U.S. EEOC (3), 2014).

> The EEOC defines religious discrimination as: Treating a person (an applicant or employee) unfavorably because of his or her religious beliefs. The law protects not only people who belong to traditional, organized religions, such as Buddhism, Christianity, Hinduism, Islam, and Judaism, but also others who have sincerely held religious, ethical or moral beliefs. Religious discrimination can also involve treating someone differently because that person is married to (or associated with) an individual of a particular religion or because of his or her connection with a religious organization or group (U.S. EEOC (3), 2014).

The two decade war in Iraq and Afghanistan has changed the world's perceptions on how they view the Muslim faith. Today, employers have mixed feelings with regards to hiring individuals from the Muslim faith. The employers' reasons do not necessarily deal with the individual's qualification, but the publicity that their company would receive from internal and external entities. As a result of the conflicts in the Middle East, Muslims have been subjected to negative stereotypes and bad treatment in the workplace.

In 2012, the EEOC sued Star Transport, Inc. because the company fired two Muslim employees after they refused to deliver alcoholic products, citing that the assignment contradicted their religious beliefs and values (EEOC (4), 2013). The EEOC stated that the employer failed to accommodate the Muslim employees, a clear violation of the religious discrimination law (EEOC (4), 2013).

Equal pay

Under Title VII of the civil rights act, the equal pay act (EPA) prohibits discrimination on the basis of sex in the payment of wages or benefits, where men and women perform work of similar skill, effort, and responsibility for the same employer under similar working conditions (CSOSA, 2014; Brenton, 2011). Equal pay advocates have longed argued that women should be paid equivalently to their male counterparts. President Obama made equal pay for women a priority in his campaign to bring closure to this issue.

Women hold top-level management positions, including CEOs and directors. However, Brenton (2011) cited:

> While an average of 20 percent wage discrepancy is certainly significant, it would be a mistake to jump on this number as proof of the persistence of sex discrimination in the workplace, because there is evidence to suggest that— much of the gap can be explained through human capital factors. Human capital is the potential—measured in terms of accumulated or acquired knowledge, experience, and skill-sets—to produce economic value through labor.

There are no significant changing views with regard to the Equal Pay Act. Today's interpretation of this law leans more toward the reverse of the 20% wage discrepancy that Brenton (2011) cited. Women are dominant in the workforce today, compared to the past perceived notion that women only wanted part-time jobs so that they would have time to take care of their families.

As discussed in Lewin's Change Model Theory, organizational leaders, employee members, and prospected members must be open to learning and adjusting to ever changing social trends, cultural norms, and behaviors in today's workforce. Over the last decade, the Supreme Court has ruled in many cases on how our traditional values and beliefs could and have resulted in legal ramifications, prompting states and private industries to reevaluate how they address civil rights situations. Politics play a major role in employment.

Chapter 3. Exercise Identify how either your civil rights have been violated or an individual close to you has had their rights violated.

	Your perceived interpretation
Age discrimination	
American with Disabilities Act	
Gender discrimination	
National origin discrimination	
Race discrimination	
Equal Pay Act	
Religion discrimination	

Chapter 4

Employment Politics

"A man without decision of character
Can never be said to belong to himself...
He belongs to whatever can make captive of him"
— John Foster, Author.

According to a Fox Business report, between 60-80% of jobs are found through personal relationships (Driscoll, 2011). We have all learned, through personal encounters or the media, how individuals obtained their jobs through some political affiliation. It has been a practice for decades where CEOs of private and nonprofit agencies would bring their own personnel or top aides along with them to a new job. This practice is more prevalent in government agencies, where executive government officials, such as the governor and agency heads (such as housing), would bring their own team of leaders whom they feel confident will help fulfill the vision and mission of the office.

Personal Motives

Many job candidates, regardless of qualifications, are rejected by an employer because of personal motives. Studies have shown that many employers interview other possible candidates as a formality and to comply with employment laws, as discussed earlier. While all along, the employer already knew who was getting the job. This dynamic will be explored further in the Illegal Employment Practice chapter.

One of the challenges that job seekers and employer's experience is trying to please everyone who may be directly or indirectly involved in the recruitment process. We have all, in many ways, been involved, either directly or indirectly, in employment politics. It is plausible that hiring managers already know who they are going to hire before the recruitment process began. How many times have you seen the following response to a job you have applied for?

Dear XXX,

Thank you for submitting your resume to XXX for consideration.

We are fortunate to have many qualified candidates apply to each of our positions. We have reviewed the qualifications of each candidate and after careful consideration, we have determined that the credentials of other candidates may better fit our needs at this time.

In many cases hiring managers may hire individuals based on recommendations, as opposed to going through the traditional recruitment process. This type of recruitment is usually done without knowing if the job candidate has the qualifications for the job. Job candidates targeted during this phase typically evade the interviewing process, in which everyone else has to participate. Job candidates who go through the interview process are placed under enormous stress to compete for the job, while the job candidate obtained through political networks does not have to endure such pressure? This method of recruitment is called the "Blind Interview."

The Blind Date and Blind Recruitment Process

A traditional date is where two individuals plan and meet at a mutual location where they can get to learn about one another. These individuals have already met and are familiar with each other. In other words, there has been some physical or mental attraction between the two parties, which made them want to explore future initiatives. Similarly, traditional interviews are designed to develop a connection with the job candidate. A second interview is scheduled if the employer feels that there can be a match between the two.

On the other hand, a blind date is arranged by a third party who has a personal connection with the two parties. These individuals, who do not know one another, only know as much information about the other party that the mutual acquaintance has revealed. The quality of such a relationship totally depends on the acquaintance's ability to match the personalities, characteristics, morals, and values of the two parties. Failure to make the right connections can erupt into a nightmare for all three parties.

Employment referrals such as job placement services and recommendations through networks are examples of blind recruitment in the employment world. There are advantages and disadvantages of blind recruitment, whether the organization is hiring internally or externally, when an employer already knows who they are going to hire, but still go through the recruitment process of having job candidates apply and interview for the already filled position.

Advantage of blind recruitment

Many employers often solicit the recommendation from internal staff on the recruitment of new employees (Schwatz, 2013). The advantage of this hiring practice is that employers may take recommendations from staff because internal employees are hopefully dedicated to the mission of the organization and would not opt to bring individuals onboard who did not share the same vision. As mentioned previously, it is assumed that the third party or staff member, who is making the connection, understands the attributes of each party before a match is made.

Schwartz further explained that large organizations, such as Ernst & Young, are using internal staff to fill vacant positions to save time and money. Moreover, companies such as Deloitte and Enterprise Rent-A-Car offers incentives and prizes to employees for their referrals. As a result, employee recommendations for Ernst & Young alone have resulted in a 45% increase of job candidates hired through internal networks.

There should not be any problems with an employer soliciting recommendations from staff members or other modes of networking to fill a vacant position, considering the goal of management is to identify the best talent to meet the needs of the organizations, hence the whole "overqualified" conversation discussed. However, the problem is the politics, which is incorporated within the recruitment. The primary concern is why do organizations post positions when they know who they will be hiring for the position?

Disadvantage of blind recruitment

Many countries, including Africa and East Asia, have preplanned marriages (Tsutsui, 2013). Arranged marriages are similar to blind dates in which the bride and the groom are selected by their perspective families and not by one another (Paquin, 2013). The disadvantage of blind dating and blind recruitment alike is that neither party is aware of whether their interests are compatible.

Studies have shown that many marriages are destroyed because the individuals later learn that they are not compatible with one another (Ahangar et al., 2013). In this article Ahangar et al. stated that when couples are married at younger ages, they are more likely to report marital conflicts, especially infidelity and jealousy. In employment terms, this younger age represents the length of time that the employer and new employee (through blind dating) have known one another and whether they are compatible. The conflicts result from the differences in personalities, characteristics, and vision that otherwise might have been detected during the traditional recruitment process, including an interview. Such outcomes may signal that the third party or internal employee did not refer a potential candidate that was compatible with the organization's needs.

Often, we are attracted by the physical appearance of what we see first, such as height, looks, complexions, fashion, and body dimensions to name a few. It is only human nature that we are attracted to these features. However, if one does not take the time to learn about the internal attributes of the person, including personality, intelligence, values, and characteristics, many problems could emerge. For example, one person may be content with only having a high school diploma, while the other promotes higher education. This difference can result in conflicts with values.

Amongst, the disadvantages of blind recruitment; the knowledge of the unknown tops the list. As previously stated, minimal information might have been shared between the organization and political referral. Crossley and Media (2014) stated that it takes longer to get a new staff member acquainted with the functioning of the organization. Finally, while the new employee might bring in new ideas, it may be a tough sell for internal staff members that are resistant to change.

It's Not What You Know, It's Who You Know

Studies show that over 45% of people stated that they got their job as a result of being referred by someone (Schwatz, 2013). This technique is the famous "It's not what you know, but who you know." There are many advantages and disadvantages to this form of hiring or courting. However, there could be legal ramifications to engaging in the blind dating method for many organizations.

This phrase has been around for decades. Let's look at each component of this phrase. The definition of "what you know" consists of the level of skills, knowledge and abilities one brings to an organization. This includes meeting the minimum qualifications for a job such as level of education, experiences and track records of performing a particular job. In general, organizations want to hire job candidates who have the expertise in helping to achieve their goals. For example, you would expect that a head chef in a restaurant would have schooling to support his knowledge, and work experience to support his abilities to perform in the profession.

While on the other hand, the definition of the "Who you know" concept consists of one's political affiliations, which in most cases appear to have more weight in the recruitment process. In many cases, it is plausible to conclude that when politics are factored into the recruitment process, that they would have more leverage over qualifications when making the hiring decision. In fact, this might be a good mixed study to explore. Loyalty is a key ingredient in the "who you know" concept. For example, the "who you know" type of leader might opt to hire someone who will not challenge the status quo, as opposed to a staff who might challenge a process.

This accepted practice, while considered ethical, has always been a question of debate. Top officials often bringing their top aides with them is a common practice. For example, Democrats and Republicans generally hire within their parties. Agency heads may bring along members who are affiliated with their perspective sororities and fraternities. The question becomes, "At which level of the recruitment process does this practice become unethical or illegal?" In other words, would this hiring practice be more acceptable while hiring management personnel?

Chapter 4. Exercise Using the job classification below, identify which hiring practices are mostly used to recruit employees.

	Hire mostly based on referrals	Hire based on qualifications
Teachers		
Food service managers		
Cable technicians		
Politicians		
Drivers		

Chapter 5

Analyzing Job Announcements

"The competition to hire the best will increase in the years ahead. Companies that give extra flexibility to their employees will have the edge in this area."
Bill Gates

Reading between the lines has contributed to added stress for job candidates responding to job announcements. Job candidates reviewing a job announcement often become intimidated and feel a little insecure about their qualifications. The combination of skills and abilities required by the employer can be daunting.

A best practice technique for easing the stress of job seekers is called Problem/Solution Comparison (PSC). The PSCs can be used by the organization and the job candidate. Without understanding PSC, it is difficult to answer an interview question, such as "What do you know about our organization?" In this session, you will learn how the organization plays the "problem" role and the job candidate plays the "solution" role.

Organizations (Problem)

In order to attract the best and brightest employees, organizations must create strategies to ensure that they not only attract those job candidates who closely match the mission, vision, and values of the organization, but keep them as well. Tony Hsieh, CEO of Zappos, stated that hiring individuals who were not a cultural fit costs the organization $100 million (Bressler, 2014).

The organization begins its dating process of attracting potential job candidates in order to form a union. Organizations interview job candidates to match their skills, knowledge, and abilities to their needs to determine if it is a fit. Should a match be made, a potential union may be formed. However, those candidates who do not meet the expectations of the organization are rejected.

When an organization begins looking for job candidates, they are looking to address their problems. They are looking for someone who can partner with them (similar to companion) to address organizational conditions. Organizations may attract hundreds of individuals who are interested in applying. However, not every candidate will fit the needed requirements. Attracting the right employee starts from the job announcement, as presented in Figure 3. Having clear and concise job descriptions and announcements can eliminate many problems.

Figure 3. Job announcement for call representative agent Call representative agent

We are looking for a call representative agent.
Responsibilities:

- Outgoing with great customer service
- At least two years of recent experience in a customer call center environment
- Successfully and consistently handle 50-100 calls a day
- Understand call center metrics
- Able to describe the details of previous call center training
- Willing to participate in ongoing coaching and training to company standards
- A solid track record of consistently and quickly producing results on the job
- A working knowledge of Windows 2007, MS Word, Excel, and Outlook, and faxing and copying equipment
- Excellent verbal and written communication skills

Figure 3: Job announcement for call representative. Adapted from Indeed.com

First we must understand what a call center representative's job is. According to onet.org, there are different titles used for a call center representative, including customer service representative, telemarketer, and telephone sales. The overall definition of a call center representative (customer service representative) is an individual who operates multiline telephone systems to address customer service concerns, or markets products and services to consumers. This position is not limited to any particular industry. The important part here is to understand how this position is customized to fit the perspective industry you are applying for.

For this job ad, the name and type of business was not disclosed, however let's assume that this advertisement was for the debt collection industry. Understanding the nature of the job and the industry will be an advantage to the job candidate. Table 2 provides a hypothetical interpretation of why the employer may require those particular skills, knowledge, and abilities.

Table 2. Interpretation of employer's requirements

Employers requirements	Interpretation
Outgoing with great customer service	I need someone who has the ability to run the company as if it was their own, while assisting me (organization) in increasing market share.
At least two years of recent experience in a customer call center environment	I am assuming that if you have two years of experience then you are able to perform adequately without supervision to serve clients
Successfully and consistently handle 50-100 calls a day	I need someone who is competitive and always striving to maintain the status quo. I really want more but I am okay with the minimum.
Understand call center metrics	I don't have the time to teach. I am assuming that if you can speak call center language then you will figure out the rest while achieving customer service goals.
Able to describe the details of previous call center training	I would like to know what strategies my competitors are using so that I can adjust my strategies
Willing to participate in ongoing coaching and training to company standards	I want someone that is teachable and willing to learn new strategies without resistance
A solid track record of consistently and quickly producing results on the job	I want someone who has the ability to do what they have to in order to achieve targeted goals and profit levels.
A working knowledge of Windows 2007, MS Word, Excel, and Outlook, and faxing and copying equipment	While these software applications are essential to the position, if your sales experience is outstanding, I will train you.
Excellent verbal and written communication skills	I want someone who sounds professional and has the gift of gab to market our products and services.

As discussed earlier, it is nearly impossible to assume that two individuals are a perfect match (solution) to one another without understanding each other's wants and needs. It is only through the dating process that each party is able to evaluate one another to determine if they are compatible. Compatibility here is equivalent to meeting the minimum qualifications (for employment), such as appearance, personality, and character.

Essentially, the organization's problem is finding someone who meets or exceeds the minimum qualifications. Organizations must ensure that the attributes they seek in a candidate are realistic. Another problem could ensue if the expectations of the job are too high. For example, it would not be necessary to require an applicant to possess a master's degree for a room service position or over 10 years of customer service experience to work a cash register. Everyone should have standards to abide by, however those standards could end up hurting the organization or individual in the long run.

Chapter 5a. Exercise Based on the five attributes listed below, provide your interpretation on what is the employer's real motive for the skill sets they seek.

Employer's requirements	Your interpretations
Someone who can work flexible hours	
At least two years of college	
Managed budgets exceeding $100,000	

Job Candidates (Solution)

The biggest challenge that job seekers face today is that an overwhelming percentage are in a vulnerable situation while seeking employment. For example, if a person is unemployed, any employment opportunity would be acceptable. A job seeker who is unemployed works tirelessly to land employment in order to address his safety needs, as depicted in Maslow's Hierarchy. Regardless of the potential conflicts with values or beliefs, it would be gratifying to have any job to address those essential needs.

Even more, most people don't like being alone. Maslow explained in his third hierarchy, a sense of belonging that people want to feel loved and accepted by others. Often, single people are vulnerable because they lack the companionship they are seeking to fulfill that need in their lives. What ends up happening is the person may be desperate to choose anyone that they think could possibly be a match. Browne (2013) stated that it makes no sense to date someone who loves kids and animals if you want a lifestyle of travel, high adventure, and risk with a partner.

A job seeker who might not be in a vulnerable situation has a job but is interviewing to obtain employment elsewhere. This individual's primary needs are satisfied and they have more control over their conditions of employment because they don't have anything to lose. They have more negotiating power and may feel more confident during the interview process. This person is confident, has a sense of belonging, and therefore doesn't need to accept just anyone. Lachmann (2013), stated that individuals who are dating should be selective and define their expectations to avoid a dating nightmare.

Given the same job description presented in Figure 1, how job candidates should approach the qualifications the employer seeks will be discussed. The art of the job hunt as the potential solution to the organization's problems is to counter each problem with a solution. Now, I am not saying to do this in a manner where you appear to be conceited. Table 3 provides an example on who how to address these problems.

Table 3. Solutions to employer's problems

Employer (Problem)	Job candidate (Solution)
Outgoing with great customer service	I have worked in retail and food service, where I worked with customers from diverse populations. In many cases, I was the lead worker to address customer concerns in absence of the manager.
At least two years of recent experience in a customer call center environment	I have 1 ½ years of experience in a call center, however within that time frame, my performance exceeded the expectation of the department and I was asked to coach new staff. In addition, I was a customer service ambassador while at company XXX
Successfully and consistently handled 50-100 calls a day	Throughout all of my places of employment, I have handled over 100 calls and face-to-face interactions daily
Understand call center metrics	I caught on quickly in learning how the call center environment worked and, as I mentioned earlier, I exceeded my daily goals
Able to describe the details of previous call center training	Reiterate the last response since they are similar in nature
Willing to participate in ongoing coaching and training to company standards	Reiterate the first and second responses
A solid track record of consistently and quickly producing results on the job	Reiterate the first and second responses
A working knowledge of Windows 2007, MS Word, Excel, and Outlook, and faxing and copying equipment	While at company XXX, I prepared reports using those software applications for over one year.

Excellent verbal and written communication skills	Reiterate on the last response. (Place emphasis on written communication). I also prepared a spreadsheet to better track our department's success and wrote a proposal to implement the spreadsheet company wide.

In many employment ads, you may experience some of the requirements overlapping. Employers might often do this to assess your qualifications from different approaches as you have seen above. The goal is to be consistent with your responses while deviating slightly to give examples of your accomplishments. For example, the last requirement was "Excellent verbal and written communication skills." Evaluate how the interviewee's accomplishments were presented to drive home their expertise.

The job candidate's answers in an interview should be collective of all jobs, situations and events pertaining to the questions unless the employer specifically asks them to focus on a particular job. The section on Interview Dynamics and Answering Interview Questions outlines how the job candidate (solution) prepares for an interview and addresses the employer (problem).

Chapter 5b. Exercise Obtain your job specifications from an employment ad (via newspaper, online). Write the requirement the selected employer is seeking in the employer's requirement's column, and counter that with how you are the solution and what you offer for that qualification as presented above.

Attributes	Employer's requirements	You offer
Education		
Skills		
Experience		
Abilities		
Other		

Chapter 6

Interviewing Dynamics

We all prospect, and don't even know we're doing it.
When you start the dating process, you are actually
Prospecting for the person you want to marry.
When you're interviewing employees, you are
Prospecting for someone who will best fit your needs.
Zig Ziglar

After decades of practice in school, community, family, social networks, and profession, individuals are still nervous on job interviews. This problem is so widespread that there are tons of publications on interviewing dynamics, which provide a guide on answering tough questions. This phenomenon is not only evident for job candidates, but for employers as well.

Likewise, there are tons of matchmaking services, and publications aimed at helping individuals choose a compatible companion. As discussed in Maslow's hierarchy of needs, if an individual has not determined what their purpose is in life (i.e family and career interest), it will be challenging for an individual to achieve self-actualization without having a vision for the future or no established standards in place to guide them. This also falls under personal branding.

There are several types of job interview and dating styles designed to match the right candidate to the job or match companions together. The goal here is to understand what style is appropriate for the situation or event. Table 4 shows the different types of interviews and dating techniques.

Table 4. Different types of interviews and dates

Types of interviews	Types of dates
Structured vs. non structure interview: A structured interview is planned and the two parties meet and the job candidate is asked prescribed questions about the candidate's qualifications (Grensing-Pophal, 2012). Non structured interviews are more open where the employer is not bound by a prescribed set of questions to uncover information about the candidate's qualifications (Grensing-Pophal, 2012).	Speed dating: A speed date is a structured matchmaking process where single men and women meet one-on-one briefly to determine if there is a potential match between the two individuals
Behavior interview: The purpose of a behavior interview, also known as situational interview, is to gage how an applicant acts and responds in certain situations (Phillips and Gully, 2013). This interview style is useful in determining if the candidate is reactive or proactive in their decision making.	Video dating: A video date is where singles have the opportunity to find a potential date by looking at video clips of individuals marketing themselves for a date.
Stress interview: A stress interview is where the employer bombards the job candidate with many questions, which may appear impossible to answer (Grensing-Pophal, 2012).	Group dating: A group date is arranged where single men and women meet and go out with the hopes of forming a partnership.
Panel interview: A panel interview, also known as a group interview, is where the employer interviews the candidate along with other company representatives to determine qualifications (Grensing-Pophal, 2012).	Blind dating: A blind date is arranged for two individuals by a mutual friend of both parties. Neither party has met each other before. The goal is that the mutual friend makes a good match.

Each interviewing and dating style has many similarities. The primary focus of these processes are to get to know the other party. In order for any of these processes to work, the individual conducting the interview must understand what they are looking for and have knowledge of the potential impact that the candidate or date will have on the internal and external surrounding they will be entering. For example, putting an employee who is not a team player in a setting where people work together, or bringing a companion around your children who is not family oriented are scenarios that are a result of what many identify as not "doing your homework."

Structured interviews have prescribed questions, such as "Tell me something about yourself," or "Why should I hire you." On the other end of the spectrum, envision individuals on a date asking one another prescribed questions from an index card. However, the interviewers are taking mental notes and comparing the responses against past dates and drawing a conclusion on who they perceive to be a better fit. A combination of structured and non-structured interviews would obtain the most information from the parties involved, as opposed to using one style.

Behavior interviews and video dating are similar in nature because the goal is to observe how an individual responds in particular situations. For example, a job candidate was asked to describe what his perception of a good boss is. A similar question was asked to a single person preparing a video, to describe what his perception of a good man is. The only difference is the face-to-face interaction.

Panel interviews and group dating are similar because several individuals evaluate how candidates respond to questions and behave in certain situations. The advantage of these interviewing styles is that one of the team members may pick up on a particular response that others may have overlooked. The disadvantage of these types of interviews is that some team members or friends may have other motives different from the company's philosophy, resulting in a conflict. For example, one might be focused on the professionalism of the individual's answers while the group members are looking at professional image.

It is no secret that most people get their jobs through others. When an employer is looking to hire someone, instead of posting the job, they may solicit a recommendation from someone in their immediate network. This is essentially a form of a blind date. The "who you know, not what you know" philosophy and blind date methods are based on trust. It is assumed that the individual making the recommendations have your best interests at heart. Otherwise, the individual making the referral would not be satisfying the employer's needs.

People are nervous during a job interview because they have not mastered the concept of branding, as will be discussed later. Human resource managers interview hundreds of job candidates a year and they still bear some nervousness. The goal of controlling your stress level is to stick to addressing the needs of the organization, to not try telling them what they want to hear, and to be true to yourself. Keep in mind, you do not have anything to lose at this point.

Chapter 6. Exercise Identify your strengths and weaknesses on each interviewing style and explain what strategies you need to employ to overcome the weaknesses in that area.

	Strengths	Weaknesses
Structured interviews		
Behavior interviews		
Panel interviews		

Answering Interview Questions

Job seekers often tell me that they can tell the employer anything that they want to hear to get the job. The truth is this philosophy is incorrect. People are smarter than that. Instead the focus should be on explaining how you would be a solution to the organization's problem. Interpreting job candidates' communication patterns, including body language, can be a factor during an interview. For example, parents are always investigating situations their children were involved in (i.e. oldest son pushed their little brother). Parents can detect if their child is fabricating what they have or have not done. Similarly, an employer's intuition can detect that there may be a problem with the job candidate's responses to questions.

The art of answering interview questions is to understand what the organization is looking for. This includes understanding the organization's industry, culture, and management style to name a few. This information falls under researching the organization in order to prepare for the interview. A best practice for preparing job seekers for an interview is to place them in the position of the employer. Doing so gives the candidate an understanding of the employer's perspective of trying to hire the right person.

This section discusses what is considered to be the five most difficult interview questions that job candidates struggle to answer. Job seekers will learn why employers ask these questions. In addition, pointers on answering those questions will be discussed. Recall the section on Analyzing Job Announcements, the key to answering interview questions is to understand what the employer is looking for in a job candidate.

What are your strengths and weaknesses?

This question is designed to depict to an employer how the job candidate's strongest skill sets and abilities would be an asset to their organization. Moreover, the employer's goal is also to assess what skills, knowledge and abilities the job candidate lack.

The key to answering this question is to focus on what strengths you have that are a necessity for the organization. For example, if you are interviewing for a telemarketing job, one of the primary functions for this job is answering phones. Therefore, you would need to elaborate on that strength. On the other hand, sales would be another key component. Your weakness may be being too aggressive while speaking to clients. The goal here is to explain what you are doing to improve on that potential weakness. Keep in mind that all weaknesses can also be considered strengths in many situations.

Where do you see yourself in 5 years?

Many organizations' goal is to create a work environment that is considered a home away from home for employees thereby maintaining a low turnover ratio. This question is designed to examine the future endeavors of the candidate and to determine if those goals are aligned with the culture that the organization is trying to create. While there is no correct way to answer this question, the key is to focus on how you plan to enhance your career, whether it is with this prospective employer or with another. Responses, such as "I want to grow with your organization" may be perceived to be desperate and telling the employer what they want to hear.

Why do you want to leave your current company?

The purpose of this question may be two-fold. First, the employer may have personal motives for asking this question. It is plausible that most individuals who seek employment usually seek employment within the same industry. From an employer's perspective, this question has the potential of soliciting information about its competitors. The employer may or may not capitalize on the information to enhance how they conduct business.

If a job candidate states that they would leave a company if there was no room for growth, then this could raise red flags for an organization that does not have room for advancement. However, if a job candidate states that they would leave an organization if they are not allowed to use their talents and expertise to achieve their goals, then this may be an advantage for an organization that is innovative and encourages employees to be creative in achieving desired outcomes.

Another reason for an employer to ask this question is to identify potential threats to an organization. The last thing an employer would want is to hire someone else's problem employee. Speaking negatively about a past employer would also raise flags for future employers because they would assume that the job candidate would provide negative feedback on them as well if they worked for them. The key to answering this question is to focus on your career aspirations and explain where you see yourself moving toward within the profession and what goals you would like to achieve.

Describe yourself

This question is asked to examine how a candidate identifies their skills, knowledge and abilities to perform the job. The question is also designed to gauge a candidate's ability to describe their character and personality. The section on personal branding will prepare you for the many possibilities for answering this question. What you don't want to do is tell your life story. The goal of answering the question is for you to describe yourself as it relates to the qualifications the employer is seeking. For example, if the job does not require home improvement as a primary function, it should not be discussed. On the other hand, your home improvement hobby would be acceptable to discuss in a situation where you are discussing creativity.

Why should we hire you?

Job candidates can also have ulterior motives for why they are seeking employment with a company. While we all have needs, as presented in Maslow's theory, the personal needs of the job candidate is not the concern of the employer. For example, hiring you because you need a job is not a sufficient reason. The goal of this question is to determine if the job candidate possesses the skills and abilities to perform the job. This question should be answered using the problem/solution theory. Again, if you cannot convince the employer that you are the solution to their hiring needs, then you are wasting their time.

Chapter 6. Exercise Identify your interpretation on why an employer might ask a job candidate the question and then record your answer based on your workplace experience.

	Employer's interpretation	Your response
How did you hear about this position?		
What were your bosses' strengths/weaknesses?		
Tell me about a time when you disagreed with your boss.		

Chapter 7

Personal Branding

"Your name and face carry your brand in both reality and virtual reality, such that wherever they are cited, your personal brand is at stake."
Dan Schawbel

It is interesting when a child is asked "What do you want to be when you grow up?" A number of occupations may emerge. As children mature and learn more about their interests and personality, their occupation becomes more definitive. Hopefully, by the time an individual has graduated from high school and enters college or trade school, they have solidified their profession. It is likely that this individual has worked in many places to gain experience and knowledge. These life experiences and events are all ingredients in helping a person to develop their brand.

Definition of Personal Branding

How we brand ourselves speaks volumes to who we say we are. Personal branding essentially involves how we want the world to see us. The best definition of personal branding is by Dan Schawbel, a Personal Branding Gen-Y Expert.

> Personal branding describes the process by which individuals and entrepreneurs differentiate themselves and stand out from a crowd by identifying and articulating their unique value proposition, whether professional or personal, and then leveraging it across platforms with a consistent message and image to achieve a specific goal. In this way, individuals can enhance their recognition as experts in their field, establish reputation and credibility advance their careers, and build self-confidence (United States Univ., 2014).

The Birth of Your Branding

According to a study published in the Journal of Extension, most children choose their career based on the influence of their parents or other family members (Ferry, 2006). For example, most children may choose to become a doctor because one of their parents is a doctor. Likewise, a child may choose to become a law enforcement agent because one of their parents or family members who they admire is a law enforcement agent. While many would use the "like father, like son" or "like mother, like daughter" saying, there are disadvantages in following another's footsteps. Personality plays a vital role in an individual's career choice.

Career counselors help individuals examine their skills, knowledge, and abilities to identify a career, which best meets their interests. In addition, there are many career assessment tools specifically designed to help individuals better understand themselves, and choose a career that best meets their interests. Even after an individual has identified their niche, they now must find a compatible workplace environment (also known as workplace culture), which will accommodate their personality and skill sets. Finding such a workplace culture requires some research from the job candidate.

Marketing 101

To analyze marketing, a great exercise is to place several brands of cereal on a table. Take a poll on which brand participants would purchase first. Usually, the majority of participants choose Kelloggs over General Mills, Post, or the store brand. On average, the justifications for the selections include factors like brand name, taste, looks, and marketing. On the other end of the spectrum, another group of participants within the same workshop utter that they would choose the store brand because the product is the same. Other comments include the packaging is different and the price is a big factor. As you can imagine, the conversations over taste and name brand usually trigger a debate between the participants.

It is challenging for small businesses and job seekers alike to identify their personal brand. What is their product or service, and what separates them from their competition? This dilemma also impacts the recruitment and selection process. Job candidates and employers must understand that recruiting the most qualified staff is two-fold. While companies want to ensure they are making the best hiring decision, job candidates should also determine if their skills, knowledge, and abilities are a good match for the organization.

Developing Your Brand

Continuing on with the cereal branding concept, consumers, generally those who are very health conscious, read the labels of products before they purchase them. The reason is simple. People want to ensure that they are only purchasing products that do not interfere with their diet plan or health.

Like job candidates, there are thousands of products on the market with similar characteristics and benefits. Some brands perform better. For example, if Tylenol advertises that their brand is rapid release, one would assume that the medicine should take affect quicker than other brands of similar medicines, such as Advil or Bayer. Likewise, an accounting firm would assume that if a job candidate is a Certified Public Accountant (C.P.A), then that candidate will follow ethical laws.

Let's assume for a moment that you were packaged inside of a box like other products. You are marketing your skill sets to employers walking down the aisle looking for a customer service representative. You are on the shelf next to other customer service candidates who are also looking to be hired. How will you stand out from your competitors? Table 5 displays descriptors that are normally presented on products about their contents and features. You will also see job interview questions that are compatible to the product's descriptors.

Table 5. Product Descriptors on Packages

Product descriptors	Comparable interview questions	General responses to descriptors
Ingredients	Tell me something about yourself? Include detailed attributes such as education, experience, certifications, and special skills	I have a high school diploma with over three years of customer service experience in healthcare, food service, and higher education institutions. I just completed a certification program for office assistants.
Instructions	Describe for me what you do on a daily basis.	I interview clients to determine what services they require and make referrals to the appropriate agencies.
Nutrition facts	How would we benefit from hiring you?	I have management and leadership qualities and experience with emphasis on training, development, and balancing budgets.
Logo	What stands out about you?	I am innovative, creative, diverse, unorthodox, a strategic planner, and a motivator
Warnings	What are your weaknesses?	I keep out of reach of organizations that are against change and don't think outside of the box.
Expiration date	What certifications do you currently hold and when do they expire?	I have a C.P.R. certification, which expires in eight months. I also have a MD state driver's licenses, which expires in five years.

The information on a cereal box is similar to a job candidate's resume, which markets them to potential employers. When consumers examine products or human resource managers examine resumes, they are both looking to determine how the product or potential employee would be beneficial to them. In addition, they are investigating what side effects or repercussions might result from the purchase of a product or the hiring of an employee. For example, if a job candidate is terminated for getting in a fight with a client. Though their actions may have been justified (they were attacked first), the employer will still label them as potentially violent.

Marketing Your Personal Image

Marketing is very important during the job search process. We often hear the phrase "first impressions are lasting." Our first impressions involve many attributes such as clothing, communication, cultural fit, personality and style. Since most participants generally choose Kelloggs over the store brand cereal because of recognition, the question posed to the group is "Are you a name brand or generic job candidate?"

The difference between a name brand and generic job candidate is the confidence level and ability of the candidate to show an employer why they would be the best choice for filling the vacancy. Mastering how to answer several branding type interview questions is a starting point to establishing your brand. The five most difficult questions that job candidates struggle to answer, which have to do with personal branding, include the following:

1) What stands out about you?
2) How would others describe you?
3) Tell me something about yourself.
4) How would this company benefit by hiring you?
5) Why are you a good fit for this job?

Updating Your Brand

In Lewin's change theory we discussed how when people are resistant to change, their behavior and beliefs may affect the productivity of the organization. Often, people might become content with what they are doing and elect not to upgrade their knowledge or keep abreast with the latest technologies. Periodically, you would even see Coca Cola change the face of its products to attract new consumers. This might be done by placing Santa Clause's picture on a soda bottle during the holiday season.

Ten steps to personal branding have been adapted from *Linked 2 Leadership: The Leadership Collaboratory*. These 10 steps include know yourself, get feedback, your talent, social media, lead by example, listen rather than hear, speak rather than talk, over commitment, and consistency. These elements are effective in terms of creating your personal brand.

Updating your brand would be equivalent to changing your attitude, personality, and work style to conform to the environment you are in. An excellent example would be a parent who communicates with other adults by normal, adult conversation. However, when they talk to their baby, they use a baby voice. Moreover, this parent might also take a parenting class to improve their parenting skills. Employers like to see job candidates who are always upgrading their skills. These trainings also look good on your resume.

Chapter 7. Exercise Identify your brand using the product descriptors below.

Product descriptors	Your attributes
Ingredients	
Instructions	
Nutrition facts	
Logo	
Warnings	
Expiration date	

Chapter 8

Developing the Resume

No one has a resume that they are 100%
comfortable with, nor does anyone have
a life that they are 100% comfortable with
Jay Baruchel

The resume is an essential tool for finding employment. Experts have long stated that the purpose of a resume is to get the interview. Job candidates are often told that there is no perfect solution to creating an award winning resume, but there are some important ingredients that should be considered. Later, you will learn the path a resume takes, from when it is received by the employer to when the organization decides to either hire or reject the job candidate.

The resume must be created with the perfect blend of ingredients, including one's skills, knowledge, and abilities that will convince the employer to explore you further. The author often refers to the resume as the appetizer to the main dish, which in this situation would be the job interview. For example, when we go through the food court in a shopping mall, one usually sees individuals passing out samples of food. These servers only give a small sample of the item they are trying to get you to buy (here, the resume).

Once the patron tastes the sample given by the server, the patron usually likes what they discover and moves to explore the food more by purchasing a meal from the restaurant. The point here is that job candidates must understand the dynamics and culture of the organization before generating a resume. Now, keep in mind that you cannot please everyone. Servers come across individuals who do not like their product and reject their offer to purchase a meal. Therefore, to be in a better position to be contacted for an interview, you should ensure that the basics ingredients, outlined below, are included in your resume.

Resume Writing Tips

One of the things that job seekers should understand while creating a resume is to not waste the employer's time by highlighting skills and attributes that any candidate should have. Such attributes only raise red flags from perspective employers. These personal statements are listed within the job duties throughout the resume; however, they are more prevalent in the resume sections often titled "Highlights" or "Summary of Qualifications."

These categories are supposed to reveal to a perspective employer attributes that convince the employer to review the entire resume. Let's go back to the dating concept as an ice breaker to make this point.

Let's visualize, for a moment, two individuals on a date. One of the individuals reveals the following attributes to his date. If in a committed relationship, I would not:

- Have an affair with another person.
- Treat your children as if they were my own.

Wouldn't you consider these attributes or qualities to be common sense for anyone who has values and morals? Similarly, when job seekers place the following attributes on their resume:

- I am a hard worker
- I am dependable
- I am a team player

Why would an employer consider interviewing a job candidate who did not meet these basic qualities anyway? This is like obtaining a high school diploma. One would assume that this individual can at least write complete sentences, and do basic arithmetic. With this said, these attributes do not provide any new information about your skills and abilities to perform the duties of the job.

Therefore, as stated above the highlight or summary of qualifications section of the resume should contain information or attributes that might enhance your qualifications and expertise for performing the job duties.

For example, I would consider the following attributes for a car sales person.

- Over 20 years of sales experience in retail, hospitality, automotive, and manufacturing industries.
- Fluent in Spanish, Sign Language, French, English, and Russian.
- Adjunct faculty of business marketing, contract compliance, and financial management.

These attributes are much stronger and gives the employer that "AH HA" or "WOW" moment they have been seeking in a job candidate. This job candidate would bring a host of diverse experience from different sales markets. They also have the knowledge and expertise to, not only explain those business concepts, but to be able to teach other sales team members strategies on improving their sales and marketing abilities. Finally, this candidate has the ability to communicate with a diverse customer base, thereby enhancing the car sales establishment's ability to communicate with a diverse population. Considering these pointers will help to enhance the quality of the resume.

Fonts

The standard fonts generally used for creating a resume are Times New Roman, and Arial. These fonts are easy to read and are friendly to the eye. The standard size of the characters is 12pt. Some individuals may use a smaller point size, say 10pt, in order to fit the resume onto one page. Other fonts may be deemed appropriate depending on the type of job one is seeking and the audience they are trying to appeal. For example, a school teacher may use other creative fonts to attract students. A chef or food and beverage manager may choose to use a font such as Script Mt Bold to make the resume look like a restaurant menu. Other fonts and point sizes may be used to show one's creative talents. Remember, there are no guidelines for the type of fonts you use, just make sure you are familiar with the organization's culture dynamics.

Styles and themes

There are many styles and themes one can use to spice up the image of their resume. There is resume software with hundreds of templates that give a particular look. However, the key here is not to use templates which do not represent the image or vision of the organization you are applying for. For example, there is a template that formats a resume in the shape of a wine bottle. While this theme may be creative for bar tenders, or in a wine brewery, it would not be appropriate for submitting to a childcare center because it could send the wrong message.

Resume length

Most resume experts say that the resume should not exceed one page. This may be true in industries which have high turnovers such as fast foods, retail, hospitality etc. However, as individuals mature in the workforce and their profession, the one page resume might not be effective, and may be a challenge for managers, directors, CEOs and college professors. Professional resumes should provide information about management, leadership, financial reporting, human resources functions, marketing, and other components that give a perspective employer an overview and track record on what you offer.

As stated earlier, the resume is like an appetizer. This appetizer must have the right kind of ingredients to give the employer a taste of what attributes the job candidate will bring to the table. The resume is essentially a compressed document, which gives the employer just enough information to let them know that you meet and/or exceed the minimum qualifications they are seeking. However, once the job candidate lands the job interview, the goal is to unzip those skills, knowledge, and abilities that were compressed. The interview will be discussed later.

Using More Than One Resume

Imagine getting a Christmas card from someone where you can clearly see that their name has been erased and your name was inserted. You might imagine the responses, such as that is unprofessional, one would not feel special, and they could at least purchase Christmas cards from the Dollar Store.

Many job candidates apply for job positions by sending the same resume. There is a problem with this practice. No different than the Christmas card situation, the employer can see that the information on the resume does not match what knowledge and skills they are seeking. Each resume must be customized and tailored to address the immediate needs of the employer. Why should an employer who is looking to hire a retail store clerk receive a resume from a job candidate looking for work in the healthcare industry?

Have someone look over your resume, preferably someone in the industry you are seeking to work, to see if you can improve the document. It would not hurt to also have individuals outside of the industry view the resume. Many people solicit the support of professional resume writers.

Using Professional Resume Services

Professional resume writers are individuals who have been trained and certified to create an award winning resume designed to get the job candidate an interview. Many professional resume writers work within one-stop career centers, college career services, and other workforce development venues catered to assist others find employment. Other professional resume writers have private practices where they work independently to create or revise resumes for their clients.

When choosing a professional resume writer, the job seeker should choose someone who is knowledgeable about the industry they are trying to enter. A lack of knowledge from the resume writer can serve as a disadvantage. Like completing a federal application, use key words that the agency may look for to get your resume top consideration. For example, there is a difference between saying "Take patients' vital signs" and "Triage patients," or "Fix cement walkways" and "Pour cast." Again, this goes back to a previous point of having the right blend of ingredients in your resume.

Job seekers need to learn how to "Speak Your Resume." Their resume should not convey something different than they convey. For example, if the job seeker is not accustomed to using certain language, then they should not use it in their resume. This would only raise questions and it sends the wrong impression to the employer during the interview. Using the blind date scenario, many individuals have been told something about a person before they actually met them only to learn later that the description did not match their observation. Therefore, the job candidate should review the resume to ensure they can speak its language and style.

Using Resume Writer Software

There is some excellent resume writer software on the market. Resume software is perfect for job seekers who do not have the expertise to create a resume from scratch. The software has many templates and formats to choose from. Many resume software have features that allow you to drag and drop job duties into the resume based on the job classification chosen. Job seekers need to understand that while some resume writer software is very useful, the content still needs to be reviewed and edited to fit a particular job. Understand that these descriptions are general in nature to give an idea of a particular task performed. For example, some descriptions may appear to be redundant.

One job duty example is "Prepare drinks from soda fountains, coffee machine, and bar." While this duty lets the job seeker know where the drinks come from, this is redundant. It would be common sense that those drinks come from some type of machinery, which makes this duty redundant. However, this duty can also be written as "Prepare alcoholic and non-alcoholic drinks." The types of machines can be discussed during the interview.

Another job duty example is "Manage and train staff, including bookkeepers, receptionists, and loan officers, in a bank to ensure that they address customer needs in a professional manner." This duty is also redundant and can be written as "Manage and train bank staff." From a management and leadership perspective, it is assumed that the purpose of training is to ensure that staff delivers quality customer service. Recall above that the resume is only an appetizer and should not contain all of the detail information.

Chapter 9

Development of the Cover Letter

"Define what your brand stands for, its
core values and tone of voice, and
then communicate consistently in those terms"
Simon Mainwaring

Similar to the creation of a resume, there is no 100% correct way to compose a cover letter. However, we still use the standard format of writing an essay. There should be a heading, date, salutation, introduction, body, closing, and signature. In doing so, you have to make the cover letter presentable and readable.

Heading

The cover letter's heading should follow the same format as the resume, for consistency. However, if you chose to use another format, your information should not deviate from the resume. For example, your telephone number should not be different. In addition, your name should not deviate. For example, if you only used your first and last name on your resume, you should follow the same format. Do not use Dr. or Ph.d or another title if you do not have the qualifications.

Date and Salutation

I have seen cover letters with dates that were totally out of sync with the job announcement someone was responding to. This might be a result of using the same cover letter for similar jobs and forgetting to change the date. Moreover, even though most job announcements don't give a direct contact name, you should do your best in attempting to find one. This is of course if the organization directly posted the job. This may not be the case if the organization used a third party and elected that the organization's name not be mentioned.

Introduction

Organizations spend thousands of dollars on recruitment and selection initiatives. They use several medias to advertise jobs. They want to ensure that they are receiving a return on their investment. If an organization learns that using a particular source to advertise jobs does not yield any results, they would discontinue using it. Therefore, it would be a good move to start your introduction by mentioning where you learned about the job. For example:

> I am writing to express my interest in the XXX position as advertised in XXX. After reviewing your requirements, my skill set fits the position you are seeking to fill. I have attached my resume for your review and consideration.

You can make the determination on if you chose to use a modified block style or indentation, as long as you are consistent. The goal of an introduction is to make it interesting enough that your reader will want to continue reading the document. Keep in mind that the cover letter introduces your resume.

The Body

In the resume section, we discussed how the resume was an appetizer. At the same time, the cover letter is the presentation of the resume. Imagine going to a restaurant and you are presented with a meal. The presentation sets the tone for what is to come. The cover letter sets the tone for the employer to decide if they want to continue to review the resume. The body should be a brief overview of what is in the resume.

The first paragraph should highlight your education, certifications, and licenses that are pertinent to the job. For example, you may have obtained a medical assistant certification, however you would not place this in the cover letter for a retail manager position. Instead, you would include your A.A. degree, non-college workshops, or classes related to management.

The second paragraph should highlight your experience doing the job. There is no need to mention the names of your jobs because they are on the resume. An example would be:

I possess over 10 year of experience in retail management, taught business courses, and created training modules. I have worked in government, private and nonprofit retail settings.

Cover Letter Style

There are two cover letter styles that I use. The first style is the traditional letter format, as discussed above. The second style is what I call the problem-solution cover letter. This involves highlighting each requirement the employer is looking for and addressing each point. A table is needed to compose this cover letter style. Keep in mind that you can make the borders transparent if you choose. An example of this cover letter style is presented in Table 6.

Table 6. Problem/solution cover letter style

You require	I offer
B.S. Degree in Management	Masters in Business Administration
Three years of management experience	Over six years of management experience in retail and food service.
Ability to work flexible shifts	As a store manager, I am accustomed to working flexible hours.

Closing

The final paragraph should highlight your accomplishments. This is your opportunity to really capture the employer's attention far more than you have done with your credentials and experience. In essence, this paragraph is what I refer to as "seal the deal." Recall earlier when I stated that a person can have all of the education and experience, but if you have not produced a track record with those attributes, it may work against you. An example would be

I have generated over $1,000,000 in sales for the northeast region, and implemented a training and

development program for new employees. In addition, I
have received several awards and recognitions.

Signature

In today's world, an overwhelming number of employment
correspondents are sent by email. Unless you are forwarding your resume
package via PDF, where you have the technology to physically sign your
name before sending the information, your typed signature is acceptable.
However, if you are sending a fax or personally submitting the resume,
you would need to sign the documents.

Chapter 10

Employment Rejections

*Rejection doesn't have to mean you
aren't good enough; it often just means the other
person failed to notice what you have to offer.*
Panda-DiVinci

Job candidates are rejected for employment opportunities by
organizations for several reasons. Many of these reasons for rejection are
identified below. While this list is not exhaustive, the top four prominent
reasons for rejection include gaps in employment, under qualification, over
qualification, and lack of culture fit.

Gaps in Employment

One of the biggest problems I have teaching a resume workshop is
when job seekers tell me they were told they have to hide their gaps in
employment so that an employer would not think that they are a job
hopper or unqualified because they have not been in the workforce for long
enough. My response to gaps in employment is that fabricating the start
and end dates of your jobs speaks more to your ethics and trustworthiness.

Let's look at this exercise I use in my class. I would ask a class of at
least 15 females if they would go out on a date with me based on what they
have learned and observed about me thus far in the class. These female
participants are considered employers for this exercise. Tell the class that
the goal is to find someone willing to date me by the end of this exercise.

Participant #1 stated that she is in a relationship.
Participant #2 stated that I was not stocky enough.
Participant #3 stated that they do not like people who wear glasses.
Participant #4 stated that she doesn't like my personality.

The point here is that you are not able to convince anyone to date me.
Therefore, I'm still left without a date. Similarly, until an employer decides

to hire me, my gap in employment will grow. An employer may want to hire you but they cannot afford the salary you want, or you may not have the type of skill sets in a particular area, or you don't look like you fit into the organization's culture. For advice on answering this question, go to the section on "Mastering the Interview."

Under Qualified

Often, employers advertise job announcements that are too vague and do not clarify the actual qualifications and abilities the employer is seeking. The goal of the employer during the employment process is to clearly explain to potential employees exactly what skill sets and qualifications they are seeking. An interview should not be conducted if there are unclear criteria. This practice could be a disadvantage for both the employer and job candidate.

For example, an organization states that it is looking for a director to manage a department of at least 100 staff members and a large budget which may exceed $500,000. These criteria are not that clearly defined as a candidate applying for this position may have managed a department of 90 staff members. While the organization may know what they mean by the language of the job announcement, the terminology of "at least" creates confusion to job candidates who will ultimately be deemed unqualified. Similarly, if this candidate works with budgets ranging from $300,000 to $550,000, this can also create confusion. Only the organization's leadership knows that they really want a candidate with the budgetary experience from $500,000 to $750,000 annually.

On the other hand, in cases where the job criteria are clearly identified by the employer, the employer would be in a better position to make a more informed decision on the qualifications of the job candidate. A job candidate may meet the minimum qualifications for a position, however the candidate may not have enough experience to be considered a good match.

Using the above example, let's say an organization is looking for a director to manage a department of 100 staff and a budget exceeding $500,000- $700,000. Because their expectations are clearly defined in terms of what they are seeking in a candidate, the organization has a clear set of standards to accept or eliminate potential candidates. Therefore, a candidate who has experience supervising a staff of 90 can easily be eliminated. What if the job candidate exceeds the expectation of the organization, should this candidate be considered over qualified?

Over Qualified

Organizations are in business to make money. The more money organizations make, the better they position themselves in the market and are able to compete. There are many organizations that are rivals and are competing for the same customer base and sales. Therefore, organizations hire the most qualified staff to help them achieve their mission. The following organizations are examples of rivalries:

- Apple vs. Microsoft
- Coca Cola vs. Pepsi
- Kellogg's vs. General Mills
- T-Mobile vs. Boost
- Ford vs. Mercedes

Periodically, these organizations opt to change personnel, from top management to line staff workers, if they do not have the skills, knowledge and abilities to put the company at the top. Let's review some of the top business restructures. Edward Records became the new chief financial officer of J.C. Penney in March of 2014 after two difficult years of financial problems. He was relocated from Houston-based Stage Stores, which operates regional department stores like Bealls, Goody's, Palais Royal and Peebles. He previously held top finance jobs at Kohl's, Belk and Federated Department Stores (Halkias, 2014).

Chris Kemp, the cofounder and chief executive of private-cloud hardware company Nebula, stepped aside to allow hardware business veteran Gordon Stitt take the chief executive position (Novet, 2013). Kemp contends that he had less experience with enterprise sales and had never been part of a public offering company (Novet, 2013).

These are just two of hundreds of stories of this nature. In each of these situations, it appears that each of these individuals (Edward Records and Gordon Stitt) were over qualified for these jobs. Why would J.C.

Penney and Nebula hire candidates less qualified to achieve their goals of advancing their organizations? This dispels the myth of "over qualified."

Therefore, if any organization uses the terminology "over qualified" during the recruitment process, I would recommend an internal examination of the management and leadership decision making process. Even in the case where an organization may not be able to afford the salary of the incumbent, this does not justify that reason for rejection. In fact, most organizations would make other arrangements, including cutting staff, to be able to afford the person. Sports teams follow this practice all of the time when recruiting top talent.

Culture Fit

Every organization has in some way established some morals, values, and practices, which governs the behavior of its members. At any time when either a current employee or potential employee display values that are not compatible with the organization's, the relationship may be in jeopardy. Cultural fit may be determined by attributes such as what school a person graduated from or what sorority or fraternity they are a member of.

Being rejected for a job can result in tremendous stress for a job candidate (Selye, 1984). Understanding the dynamics of these rejections will give job candidates a better insight on what may happen during the employment decision making process. This stress will be discussed in the chapter on "Job Stress." Moreover, being rejected from a possible employment opportunity may actually work to the job candidate's benefits.

Chapter 10. Exercise Identify three jobs where you have been rejected for employment. Explain how each of these attributes might have contributed to the rejection and provide a justification that if presented to the employer, they might reconsider you.

	1st job rejection	2nd job rejection	3rd job rejection
Gaps in employment			
Under qualified			
Over qualified			
Cultural fit			
Challenge the rejection			

Chapter 11

The Job Developing Process

"If you can hire people whose passion intersects with the job,
they won't require any supervision at all.
They will manage themselves
better than anyone could ever manage them.
Their fire comes from within,
not from without. Their motivation is internal, not external."
Stephen Covey

Human resource management is essentially known as the people's department of the organization. Human resources (HR) address any issues related to employees from the initial recruitment to retirement. You would typically hear the term "Human Resources Manager" for small businesses or "Department of Human Resources" for large organizations. This chapter will only address the recruitment and selection process to give job seekers an overview on what goes on behind the scenes. This is once you have hit the send button to apply for a job online or directly pass your application or resume off to an HR manager.

Before jumping into the recruitment and selection process, it is important to reveal the processes that occur leading up to it. This development of the job actually starts at the inception of the business. The recruitment and selection process generally starts once the organization posts the job to the public. Each of these components will be explained.

Entrepreneurship

Organizations are born each year with the primary focus of providing a product or service to satisfy the wants and needs of consumers. In addressing those wants and needs, organizations develop strategies that will give them the advantage over their competition and create a monopoly in the product or service offered. Different levels of employees and management structures are created to ensure that the organization maintains its market position. Maintaining a competitive edge requires hiring a workforce with the skills, knowledge, and abilities to assist the organization's growth.

Now, picture yourself in the position of the entrepreneur. If you are trying to satisfy consumers and grow your organization, would you tell an applicant that they are "over qualified" to help you reach your goal (something to think about)? Once the owner or organization establishes their business strategy, a job analysis is performed.

Job Analysis

According to US Legal (2014), job analysis is a systematic study of jobs to determine what activities and responsibilities are included, their relationships with other jobs, the personal qualifications necessary for performance of the jobs, and the conditions under which work is performed. In terms of a relationship, this is the phase where you determine what you are looking for in a soul mate. For example, the employer has determined that he wants his customer service representative to have a minimum of three years of experience, a C.P.R. certification, and one-year of experience working with youth. Likewise an individual might require their soul mate, as discussed earlier, to be at least 40 years of age before they would entertain dating the person. Recall that this criteria has to do with what minimum competencies are expected to satisfy the employer's need.

Organizations use a collection of data analysis to help them determine what competencies are needed to perform a task (OPM, 2014). Information from a job analysis can also be used to determine job requirements, training needs, and position classification. For example, when factoring the level of education required for a customer service manager job, an organization might compare what knowledge is needed to perform the job against knowledge gained from associated levels of education. Table 7 gives an example of what knowledge and skill sets might be gained on each education level.

Table 7. Description of educational skill sets

High school diploma	Associates of arts degree	Bachelor's degree
Basic reading, writing and arithmetic competencies. An overview of the career occupations.	Principles of management, including human resources, accounting and marketing	Analyzing business systems and processes to provide critical thinking and strategic planning to correct the issues.

Let's say that the minimum knowledge an organization wants the job candidate to have is to be able to motivate staff, address customer concerns, and generate sales reports. Some organizations, such as small to medium sized businesses, might argue that a high school diploma is acceptable to do the job. However, a larger organization might require the job candidate to have an AA degree. A bachelor's degree may not be needed for this particular job because the organization has already determined a salary range for individuals in this classification. Hiring or considering an individual with a higher educational level than required might result in management exceeding its projected salary budget.

Let's not get the job analysis confused with the so called "over qualified" label. Most hiring managers might state that the job candidate is "over qualified" because the education requirement outlined in the job analysis exceeds the education requirements. However, the hiring manager's concern might be their ability to pay a higher salary for higher education. If the goal of an organization is to convince job candidates to work for them, it would not be attractive for an organization to tell candidates that they cannot afford their salary. Therefore, they would rather put a positive spin on the rejection that the job candidate is over qualified for the position, thus avoiding a negative reputation.

Job Description

Job description refers to the required tasks, knowledge, skills, abilities, and reporting structure required for a position. Typically, job descriptions are used for advertising an open position, determining compensation, and as a basis for performance reviews. Salary surveys are always based on descriptions and specifications US Legal (2) (2014). Many small businesses do not produce job descriptions due to time constraints. In cases where the owners have to handle many operational functions, they may not have time to compose this, as opposed to a larger organization where the human resources department handles this responsibility.

In essence, the job description provides a breakdown of the job responsibilities, as well as the education and skills required to perform the job. O*Net provides an overview of the competencies that are required to perform a specific job, including tasks, knowledge, work activities, and work values to name a few. Job descriptions are derived based on the information in the job analysis. Once the position has been created the next step is to advertise the job position.

Chapter 12

The Recruitment and Selection Process

"Recently, I was asked if I was going to fire an employee
who made a mistake that cost the company $600,000.
No, I replied, I just spent $600,000 training him.
Why would I want somebody to hire his experience?"
Thomas J. Watson Sr.

The recruitment process occurs once the job description has been approved by management and a position is now open for employment. Many organizations might open up the position internally first before opening the position to the general public. Advertisement of the position starts with the presentation of a job announcement or employment ad.

Job Announcement

The job announcement is the last document generated, which is a further breakdown of the job requirements. These advertisements are publicized through many medias, including websites, job boards, newspapers, and word of mouth. These job ads are designed to attract job candidates to an organization. Like advertising products and services, HR managers have to employ similar marketing strategies to recruit the most qualified applicants.

Usually, employers start a job announcement by giving an overview of their organization's functions and by highlighting some of their accomplishments. Then, the job position and responsibilities are outlined. Afterwards, the company explains how hiring an individual with the necessary skill sets would benefit their organization. Finally, the last step is the part that sells the job to the candidate. The organization outlines how the candidate will benefit by joining their organization because of its compensation package. If the recruitment campaign is effective, job candidates will apply and submit resumes.

Prescreening

Hauenstein (2010) defined the pre-screening process as it relates to the initial evaluation of candidate qualifications at the time of application. The purpose is to reduce a potentially large candidate pool to a more manageable number that can progress to phases of more rigorous assessment. This is what I call the HR strainer process. During the prescreening process, HR sends resumes and applications through several rounds in the strainer. These rounds may not necessarily be in any particular order.

Round one (application)

Many job candidates set themselves up for elimination by not following the instructions to apply. For example, if you are requested to submit a cover letter with the resume and you fail to do so, expect your information to go to the junk pile. Moreover, if a candidate does not submit the application package before the deadline, you can also expect your information to go to the junk pile. This is the first stage of the strainer process. Only those applicants who have followed the submission process will advance to the next round.

There is one point is worth reiterating here. As mentioned, many resume writers have been expressing that placing an objective on a resume is obsolete. Let's reexamine the submission process. If a large organization has hundreds of application and resumes, without placing the position you are applying for on the application or within the objective on the resume, how would HR know which department to filter the resume to? This resume will end up in the junk pile with the other rejected applicants.

Round two (minimum qualifications)

Round two involves analyzing the job candidate's skill set against the minimum qualifications required. For example, as discussed above, if the organization is seeking a candidate with an AA degree and two years of experience in accounting, and the candidate only poses one year of accounting experience, this candidate will most likely be eliminated from the pool. Keep in mind that these rounds of eliminations are only based on the data presented in the applications. There is no human interaction during this phase.

This is why it is very important to clearly define why you meet the qualifications. A position in the federal government is a perfect example of how many applicants may be eliminated for failing to provide the needed information. Those job candidates who survived round two, the prescreening process, progress to the interviewing stage of the recruitment and selection process..

Interviewing Process

A job interview is a process in which a potential employee is evaluated by an employer for prospective employment in their organization (Hauenstein, 2010). The interview is usually the first face to face interaction between the employer and job candidate. You are now on stage. It is your job to keep your audience engaged and impressed by your skill set. Job candidates are told that if they are called to participate in a job interview that the job is already 80% theirs. That 80% consists of passing the prescreening process. However, the remaining 20%, though it appears to be a low percentage, is the toughest to pass starting with the first interview. This 20% involves the face to face interaction.

First interview

The first initial interview is very critical. The job candidate's internal and external attributes are under review. Similar to dating, if one of the parties do not find the other attractive or if the job candidate does not fit the image an employer has for a particular job, then they won't be chosen. The job candidate's image sets the tone for the interview. For example, a woman with unnatural color in her hair is interviewing for an administrative position. She would not fit the image of an individual in that position. Moreover, studies have shown that short men are not perceived as strong leaders. Therefore, a gentleman who is interviewing for a Director's position may not be taken seriously.

The goal is not to discourage anyone during an interview; it is merely to explain the psychology, which may surface behind the scenes. As discussed previously, you cannot please everyone, however you can try to eliminate as many negative variables as possible, such as unnaturally colored hair, unprofessional attire, or fragrance. It is always a good sign when the job candidate is called back for a second interview. The first interview accounts for about 12% of the remaining 20%.

Second interview

The second interview should be less stressful for the job candidate compared to the first. The job candidate has made it through the prescreening process and the first interview. The management team is very impressed with you. At this point, the organization has already deemed you as a good cultural fit. Depending on the size of the organization, the second interview may be the final interview before a selection is made.

Usually, the second interview is with upper management personnel. While the first interviewing team has informed the second tier team that you are a good fit, they may still have some challenging questions to validate your fit. Keep in mind that there might be more candidates who have made it to round two. You are not out of the woods yet. The remaining 8% has to do with top management's assessment of you. For non-management positions, department managers and store manager might be the second tier personnel. For management positions, the second tier may be Directors, Vice-Presidents, Presidents, CEOs or a Board of Directors. Once you make it pass the second interview, you should receive a call to proceed in the process.

Background Check

Generally, when an organization states that they are going to do a background check, most people usually associate a background check with a criminal background. A criminal background investigation is not the only record that organizations check. The following records can be requested by employers. These records include the following, though this list is not exhaustive:

- Civil Records
- Credit Report
- Criminal Record

- Driver's Records
- Education Records
- Licenses and Certifications
- Medical Records
- Military Records
- Personal References
- Political Records
- Social Media
- Substance Abuse
- Worker's Compensation

It is conceivable that criminal backgrounds and credit reports present the most problems for job candidates. This is because many employers are too critical and rush to judgment while analyzing these reports. These two reports can present internal and external problems for the organization's stakeholders. Depending on the situation and events surrounding the hiring decision, an organization can be heavily scrutinized based on their discretion.

For example, the organization's requirement might request that a job candidate's credit report cannot show any delinquency within the last 10 years to qualify for employment. Job candidate "A" might have 12 years of non-delinquency and job candidate "B" might have 16 years free of delinquency. Candidate "B" might show a high balance on a credit card. Though both of these candidate's meet the requirement for employment, the HR manager might eliminate both candidates because candidate "A"s delinquency is too close, and candidate "B"s close to maxed credit card might signal poor budgeting skills.

Moreover, an organization's requirements might state that a job candidate cannot have any felonies within the last 10 years. Candidate "A" does not have a criminal background at all. However he was charged with possession of narcotics, of which the court found him not guilty. An employer might use this information to conclude that this person is involved in illegal activities, thereby eliminating him from the pool of candidates. Both situations are heavily based on the discretion of the HR manager reviewing the information.

These background checks should be a breeze for most job candidates, especially those who don't have anything to hide. Again, understanding which credentials or records an employer will be checking will be helpful in ensuring that you will meet their expectations. Many employment sectors and industries may verify records that may not be a necessity for others. For example, unless a job requires a person to drive a vehicle, there would be no purpose for requesting a driver's record. Likewise, unless a job candidate will be working with money, there would be no reason to request a credit report. Passing the background checks almost always secures you a job.

Job Offer

The job offer consists of the organization making an offer to you to accept employment at their establishment. You have met all of the employer's expectations and have passed the background checks. You have made it to the door of your future employer. But, not so fast, you are still not in the door yet. You still have the option of accepting or rejecting the job offer. Provided that you accept the job offer, you still have one phase to complete before you step through the door.

Compensation and Incentive Package

A compensation package is the combination of benefits that an employer offers to employees. This package may include wages, insurance, vacation days, guaranteed raises, and other perks. Organizations may deviate from its standard benefit package depending on how interested they are in hiring the job candidate. In this situation, it is good to know how to negotiate your salary.

Again, the job candidate still does not have their foot in the door yet. The two parties have to negotiate a compensation package. The employment process can end here if both parties do not agree on a package. Let's assume that the job candidate accepts the compensation package offered. This would be the equivalent of two individuals getting engaged. Congratulations, you are now a member of our organization.

Probation Period

The probationary period would be equivalent to how couples address situations while they are engaged. You are still in the strainer at this point, waiting to be shifted into the organization as an official employee. We often hear how people change during this stage of engagement. Both parties have begun to let their guard down gradually and become more comfortable with one another. This stage is the most critical as both parties are introduced to untapped areas of each other's lives, such as learning more about their personalities, behavior patterns, and other attributes that might present red flags.

Likewise, a job candidate might have passed all layers of the screening process leading to employment, but they still must demonstrate that they can practice what they preach in more personal encounters. The organization is watching the candidate's every move and may impose some stressful tactics on them to analyze how they would respond should a particular situation present itself. If the organization deems that the candidate (now employee) can not handle the responsibilities of the job or is not a good cultural fit, among other factors considered, the organization may elect to terminate employment.

Recall earlier, we discussed how both parties were examining if they should form a lasting relationship with the other. The job candidate is examining the organization to determine if they live up to the image that they portray to the public. For example, an organization publicizes that they promote from within. However, you uncover while working on the inside is that, while the organization does promote from within, the percentage is only a fraction of their external hires. At this point, within the probationary period, the job candidate (now employee) can decide whether they want to remain a member of an organization that portrays the wrong image.

Final Employment Determination

Many organizations do not start the employee's benefit package until they complete their probationary period. This is based on the terms of the compensation package. Let's say that you are approaching the end of your probationary period and it is determined that both parties are comfortable with one another. It is time to walk down the aisle to an official marriage.

Saying the words "I do" is equivalent to arriving at work the day after your probationary period ends. Your employer meets you at the door or comes to your office and congratulates you on completing your probation. You are now an official member of the organization, have full access, and can take advantage of all benefits that other employees enjoy. This is a good feeling. Some large organizations might have a celebration for the employee, while other employers might issue a monetary award to the employee and the placement agency (if one was involved in the recruitment phase) for their referral of a qualified candidate.

Chapter 12. Exercise Consider your last three employment opportunities, identify where in the recruitment and selection phase you felt that you did not measure up to the employer's expectations. Next, explain what corrective actions you will take in the future to avoid the same blunders.

	1st job opportunity	2nd job opportunity	3rd job opportunity
Analyzing job specs			
Application process			
Min qualifications			
First interview			
Second interview			
Background check			
Job offer			
Incentive package			
Probation Period			
Final Offer			

Chapter 13

Employers Market vs. Employee's Market

"Focus on a few key objectives ... I only have three things to do.
I have to choose the right people, allocate
the right number of dollars,
and transmit ideas from one division to
another with the speed of light.
So I'm really in the business of being the
gatekeeper and the transmitter of ideas."
Jack Welch

An employer's market versus an employee's market is a very interesting concept to explore. The housing market is sometimes used as an example when discussing the difference between an employer's market and employee's market. However, there may be other terms such as labor market trends, or a job market. Understanding the difference between the employer's market versus an employee's market may put the job seeker in a better position to negotiate for employment incentives.

First, let's explain how the housing market works. In the housing market, there is a buyer and a seller. The buyer is an individual or individuals who are in the market to purchase a home or some type of property for either a business venture or a private home (Coldwell Banker, 2014). The seller is the individual or individuals who sell real estate. These individuals would include a realtor, private home owner, or real estate agency that represent the property owner for whom they are attempting to sell the property (Coldwell Banker, 2014).

Employee's Market

An employee's market and a buyer's market have similar characteristics. A buyer's market is where there is more real estate available than the demand (Coldwell Banker, 2014). This means that there are more property owners looking to sell their property and less people interested in purchasing property. In this situation, the property owners have to market their property in a manner to attract potential property purchasers. This may include lowering prices, adding amenities, or paying for part of the purchase.

Similarly, an employee's market is where there is a large supply of employees with the skill set, education, experience, and expertise within a particular industry. However, the demands for such employees are scarce. In this situation, the organization has the upper hand in terms of the conditions of employment.

For example, potential employees may be compelled to accept a lower compensation package and commit to an increase in their workload. Moreover, the employer may be in a better position for requiring individuals to have expertise in other areas for the same salary. Let's assume that a firm is recruiting a Chief Financial Officer (CFO). Because the market is flooded with CFOs looking for work, the firm may also attach Human Resource functions to the job duties in order to save salary. This situation most definitely places the job candidate at a disadvantage.

According to the United States Department of Education, the U.S. is currently experiencing a shortage of teachers for K-12 in the public school system (U.S. Department of Education, 2014). This shortage of teachers makes this an employee's market because the school systems are offering all types of incentives, including tax credits and home purchasing assistance for those teachers considering to move to a geographical area (U.S. Department of Housing and Urban Development, 2014). New teachers, in this situation, would have an advantage in the negotiation of a compensation package.

Employer's Market

An employer's market and a seller's market also have similar characteristics. However, an employer's market and a seller's market are the opposite of the employee's and buyer's market. In a seller's market, the demand for property or real estate is greater than the supply (Coldwell Banker, 2014). Therefore, sellers have the advantage where they can raise the price of their property since buyers are competing to make the purchase.

The seller in this scenario is the job seeker or potential employee with the skills, knowledge and expertise that employers are seeking. Employees within this category are scarce and often hard to recruit. Given this challenge, the employer may offer incentive packages and sign-up bonuses to compete with rival organizations to attract the most qualified individual. This also supports the point illustrated earlier in the section "Over Qualified."

Examples of individuals in the hardest to recruit classifications might include funeral home directors, surgeons, and software engineers. This is not to say that other positions such as a CEO, marketing manager, or sales clerk may not be hard to find. The point here is that if you have the skills and expertise that a perspective organization is seeking, then you may receive offers to work for them.

Sports agents market players as hot commodities forcing team owners to bid for the player. Usually, the team which puts forward the most attractive incentive plan and compensation package usually wins the recruitment war. Job candidates in an employer's market have the ability to negotiate salaries and other compensation packages.

Chapter 13. Exercise Using the job classification in the chart, explain which entity you believe fall under employer's and employee's market. Justify your answers.

	Employer's market	Employee's market
Veterinarians		
Funeral home directors		

Chapter 14

Salary Negotiation

*"You're in a much better position to talk with
people when they approach you than when you
approach them."*
Peace Pilgrim

One of the most difficult questions to answer on a job interview besides
the traditional "Tell me something about yourself" is "What salary are you
looking for?" Many organizations also require that job candidates submit
a letter with their salary requirements, or they may be required to include
the information on the application. Often, individuals may use responses
such as, salary is negotiable or will discuss during the interview.

The challenging part of answering salary related questions for most
job candidates is that they don't want to make it appear that they are
asking for an amount which is totally outside of the range of what the
company is offering. For example, the company may be paying from
$50,000 to $60,000 for the position. However, if the job candidate
asks for $70,000, he may be eliminated from the pool of applicants.
Moreover, asking for a salary that is below what the organization is
paying may raise red flags. While on one end of the spectrum, asking
for a salary below $50,000, let's say $43,000, would definitely save the
organization in salary costs, an employer may consider your low offer as
not being qualified.

Pricing/Salary Schematics

Depending on the type of job, such as HR or payroll, an employer
may want to question your credibility for the job. Some applicants may
simply play it safe by giving a salary range such as $40,000 to $55,000.
This strategy may buy them time until they meet with the employer. The
real question here is how can a job candidate negotiate their salary without
having the knowledge or resources to do so? Job seekers place themselves

in a vulnerable position when the employer is left to determine what salary they should be paid.

As a segue into salary negotiation, let's examine how market prices are developed for new products. When new products are introduced to the market, such as cereal, prices are usually based on the going prices of comparable cereals. For example, if Kellogg's sells a large box of its famous Frosted Flakes for $4.99 and a small box for $2.99, then that is the set market price range for name brand cereal. Once a new manufacturer introduces a new cereal to the market, the goal is to create a consumer base. So, you might see the prices of the new cereal priced slightly lower than the existing Frosted Flakes brand so they can establish a customer base before raising prices.

Estimating one's salary or self-worth for a job uses a similar methodology. According to Rangwala (2012), finding out what you are worth requires research, self-reflection and networking. U.S. Bureau of Labor Statistics provides data on salary scales for different job occupations and industries. However, for the purpose of this model, I will use a nationally recognized assessment tool called the Occupational Information Network (O*Net) to demonstrate how to determine an appropriate salary.

O*Net Online

O*Net is a free online database that contains hundreds of occupational definitions to help students, job seekers, businesses and workforce development professionals understand today's world of work in the United States (O*net online, 2014). In other words, O*net provides information on the skills, knowledge, and abilities to do a job (O*net online, 2014). For the purpose of this publication, Wikipedia provides a better breakdown of O*net's layout of features. Wikipedia outlines the features as follows:

- Personal requirements: the skills and knowledge required to perform the work;
- Personal characteristics: the abilities, interests and values needed to perform the work;
- Experience requirements: the training and level of licensing and experience needed for the work;

- Job requirements: the work activities and context, including the physical, social, and organizational factors involved in the work;
- Labor market: the occupational outlook and the pay scale for the work;

Navigating o*net

O*Net is a starting point for helping job seekers create a salary inquiry, which some employers may require as part of the application process. You can connect to this site from the following link http://www.onetonline.org. Once you search for your career occupation (let's say food service manager), you will be presented with a list of similar job titles. Choose the title that best fits your requirements. For this example, let's use the first option (food service managers).

Once you open the link to food service managers, scroll down to the section titled "Wage and Employment Trends." You will find the average wage for that position. What is also good to note in this section is the number of job vacancies that are in this field.

In Chapter 13, we discussed the employer's versus the employee's market. Looking at the number of vacancies in this field, one may conclude (given other data such as geographical location and a more definitive number of available jobs) which entity controls the market. Once you identify the state you will work in (for this example, Maryland was selected), you can examine the average salary ranges.

You will get an idea of what the average employer is paying in your state compared to the national average. If you are a regional director or hold a position where you work in large geographical areas, you might want to negotiate a salary which falls between the local and national pay scale. If you really want to improve your salary negotiation abilities, you might also want to visit the Bureau of Labor Statistics (http://www.bls.gov/home.htm), and further explore trends and data about the industry and job you are targeting. Aligning the salary data against the minimum qualifications is essential for identifying a salary.

Minimum Qualifications

For the purpose of explaining minimum qualifications, we will often refer back to Chapter 4, where we discussed analyzing job announcements. An employer may require the job candidate to have the following skills or credentials to be considered for a front desk position in a hotel:

- High school diploma;
- Two years of hotel experience;
- One year of cashier experience;
- Exceptional customer service experience;
- Knowledge of surrounding areas and landmarks;

Those attributes as outlined by the organization are the minimum knowledge and experience required. Recall that the minimum qualifications for a particular job classification are outlined in the job analysis section. Why are these attributes important when determining one's salary? Here is an example of an exercise I use in my classes to demonstrate how to determine the minimum qualifications.

Job seekers should be able to answer "What is the lowest age of an individual you would consider dating?" I also ask, "What is the highest age you would consider dating?" Let's say that a 33 year old participant stated that she will not date anyone under 30 years old and no one over 45 years old. At least 90% of students reference "maturity" as the reason for the lowest age they would consider dating and that a person below that age has not matured enough for them.

On the other hand, participants overwhelmingly would agree that dating anyone past a certain age span would indicate that the individual is already set in their ways and would not be willing to compromise or change. These scenarios are equivalent to how organizations determine what skills, knowledge, and abilities are needed to meet the level of maturity for a position. Minimum qualifications are established for education, experience, and other skills, which are essential to the job.

Challenging the Status Quo

Many job seekers disqualify themselves from the applicant pool because they have not mastered the art of deciphering that they might not possess the minimum qualifications prima facie. However, the job candidate may in fact possess those qualities and skills the employer seeks. To drive this point home, let's revisit the minimum age requirement scenario presented above.

Recall that in my workshop exercise that many individuals have stated they would not date a person whose age is less than their requirement. The perceived reason is that anyone who falls below the age level has not reached the desired maturity level. This assertion might in fact have the reverse outcome. For the most part, we generally assume that once an individual reaches the age of 18 that they suddenly mature into an adult and no longer act like a child or engage in childish activities. On the other hand, we have met teenagers who matured into adulthood before they reached 18.

This is why I tell job seekers, "Not So Fast." Going back to the personal branding section, you need to own your skills. Dag Hammarskjold, Nobel Peace Prize Winner, stated, "Never for the sake of peace and quiet deny your own experience or convictions." You may not have reached the ideal criteria recommended by the employer, but you could have outperformed your counterparts, and been given increased responsibilities within your short time in the position. Again, I also tell job seekers that education and experience do not mean anything unless you are using it wisely. Let's look at two scenarios.

For example, an employer is looking for a manager with at least an Associates of Arts degree in retail management. The owner might conclude that if the candidate holds this degree then he could use sound judgment, have good troubleshooting skills, and have the leadership skills to lead the staff. Many job candidates may have the knowledge and skills the employer is seeking. However, they do not have the educational credentials. This is where all of those areas we have discussed in Chapters 4, 5, and 7 come into play.

Remember, this employer has a problem that needs to be addressed. The solution is not necessarily the degree, but rather whoever can perform those duties as outlined. A job candidate who possesses these skills, but only holds a high school diploma, is motivated to highlight their skills, knowledge and abilities in retail management. Marketing is the key here. You have to separate yourself from the pack and stand out. Understanding where your skill set falls within the parameters of the employer's expectations is very important when determining your salary range.

The Pay Rate for Knowledge and Skills

When I'm facilitating a resume or interviewing workshop, one of the things I notice is the number of participants who do not include other duties and responsibilities carried out at their previous jobs. For example, many individuals have performed tasks outside of their job specification; let's say a retail sales clerk. While this employee is not a manager, they have in many capacities performed core management duties such as making bank runs, managing shifts, and opening and closing the establishment. Most job candidates do not include these duties because it might make them appear to be a manager, when that wasn't their job title.

Wrong Answer; if you have acquired skills and have performed them regardless of the position you currently hold, get paid for them. Otherwise, the new employer might under estimating your worth. Again, match your skills against the minimum qualification of what the employer is seeking. For starters, I would use the average minimum local or national starting salary for the perspective job and work your way up based on how much you feel you should be paid for the position.

Keep in mind that those salaries are only averages. Some of the employers might pay lower than the average and you may discover that the job might not fit your pay scale. Research on the industry and salaries is important. You would not only save time applying, but also interviewing for the job knowing that it will not pay you what you are seeking.

Chapter 14. Exercise. Find a job ad that you are interested in applying for from one of your media sources (Indeed, Linkedin). Next, log onto O net. Obtain the information about your job (i.e. manager, marketing, food service). Complete the following information. Recall the information you have learned in earlier chapters to help complete this assignment.

	State projected wage		Federal projected wage		Your projected wage	
Position	Starting salary	Salary cap	Starting salary	Salary cap	Starting salary	Salary cap

Justify why you should be paid the projected salary you identified. Remember, start with the minimum qualifications that the employer is requiring and compare those against what you offer, as explained in Chapter 5.

Chapter 15

Job Search Stressors

*"How we perceive a situation and how we
react to it is the basis of our stress.
If you focus on the negative in any situation,
you can expect high stress levels.
However, if you try and see the good in the situation,
your stress levels will greatly diminish."*
Catherine Pulsifer

One of the questions I ask participants at the beginning of an interview workshop is "How many people are nervous during a job interview?" Usually about 80% of participants raise their hand. I then ask; "What makes you nervous during this process?" On average, I generally get the following responses:

- Trying to make the first impression lasting is stressful;
- Trying to ensure that I convince the employer that I really want the job;
- Hoping I prove that I have the experience to do the job;
- Hoping that they don't ask me to tell them something about myself;
- Explaining how I would be a good match for the job;
- Explaining gaps in my employment;
- Discussing past work relationships with past employers;
- Discussing why I want to leave my current place of employment.

The amount of stress that we place on ourselves when we have to talk about us is enormous. It might seem to be silly but, it is amazing how we freeze up when we have to talk about ourselves. While we may experience some stress when creating a resume, the most stress during our job search emerges during the job interview.

Going back to the dating analogy, we tend to be nervous while dating because most people place too much emphasis on trying to say the right thing. Moreover, most people fear being rejected. Most stress can be avoided while dating or interviewing if we learn to have confidence in ourselves, and learn to say what is honest and appropriate instead of the "right" thing. For example, an employer asks you if you are available to work overtime. You reply yes so that you can get the position. However, because of childcare arrangements, you knew that working overtime would be a challenge. In this situation, a better response might be, "I'm not available but, if you give me at lease a one-day notice I can make arrangements."

Selye's Stress Theory

Hans Selye's general adaptation syndrome (GAS), also known as the stress syndrome, is an interpretation of how the body confronts stress (Selye, 1984). In hindsight, such stressors emerge when people try to live outside of their means or attempt to fit the description of someone else who doesn't fit their true self. As discussed in Chapter 8 in the cultural fit section, you cannot please everyone. Trying to do so will only intensify your stress. Individuals who are unaccustomed to being in stressful situations may experience serious health problems (Selye, 1984).

Selye identified three phases that the body experiences while trying to address the stress. These phases include the following:

- Alarm reaction to stress;
- Resistance to stress;
- Exhaustion from stress.

Alarm reaction to stress

The first phase of Selye's stress theory is called the alarm reaction, also known as the fight or flight phase. Job seekers spend hours preparing for a job interview. They may engage in mock interviews or attend workshops. You are now sitting, waiting to be called in for your interview. You name is called, you are next; your natural instinct now kicks in.

The result may be what Selye (1984) has described as the fight or flight stage. During this phase, the body prepares itself for the excitement of the stressful event (Selye, 1984). Under normal conditions the body maintains a balanced state of health until stressful events emerge (Selye, 1984). The body produces an adrenaline rush as the fight or flight response (Selye, 1984).

The stress syndrome is caused by anticipating what questions the employer might ask you or the questions that you don't want them to ask you. Lazarus (1966) has stated that the lack of control over processes may result in the presence of stress for individuals. It is plausible that job candidates during the interview may feel powerless and that the interviewer has control over their life during those intense moments. Confronting the root cause of the stress, which may be the lack confidence, is key during this first stage as the body prepares itself to defend against future stressful events (Selye, 1984).

Resistance to stress

Selye (1984) has identified the second phase of the stress theory as the resistance phase, where the immune system puts up a defense to assist the body in reducing stress. The immune system produces an adrenaline rush during the fight or flight response (Selye, 1984). In this case, as the interviewer asks questions, many of us would evade the question by attempting to tell the employer what they wanted to hear to ease the stress level.

When an individual is constantly subjected to stressful situations, their body is exposed to many physiological disorders, including cancer, diabetes, and a breakdown in the immune system (National Institute for Occupational Safety and Health, 2011). According to the National Institute for Occupational Safety and Health (2011), healthcare costs have skyrocketed due to workplace stress. I consider the interview phase as workplace stress because we experience similar stressors while on the job and trying to prove to the employer that we can do the job.

The best solution to combat this syndrome is to learn more about yourself and to increase your level of confidence. In my workshops, I prescribe 30 minutes of looking in the mirror daily. I use a strategy that I call the Mirror Test. Stand in front of the mirror and speak five positive attributes about yourself that you want employers to know. It never fails. The first time that you do it, I would almost assure you that you will feel a level of discomfort, and you may silently state how stupid you look. This resistance is only your self-esteem and lack of confidence speaking.

Exhaustion from stress

The final phase of Selye's stress theory is exhaustion (Selye, 1984). The lack of preparation for a job interview, as highlighted in Chapters 4, 5, and 7, can cause stress. If you walk into a situation or event blindly, you are promoting a self-inflicted stressful situation. For example, the U.S. Army has been able to enter into other countries and capture leaders such as Bin Laden, and Sadan Hussain with minimum detection from their citizens. Such operations would not have been successful without understanding how the opposition works.

Exhaustion is the result when the body becomes overloaded or burned out, and experiences adrenal fatigue or dysfunction (Selye, 1984). According to Selye, (1984), exhaustion is the most dangerous phase of Selye's theory on stress because chronic stress may ensue, which results in internal damage to the body. It is possible that this stage of stress for job seekers emerges at the point when they are on stage to interview for the job and all of their confidence suddenly goes out of the window. I have heard of many stories from job seekers where they have broken down and cried, or fainted because they could not handle the stress of the interview.

To avoid such stressors during your job search, it is recommended you solicit the assistance of career professionals that are trained to assist you, starting from the initial phase of completing the job application to accepting the job offer. If these conditions go unaddressed for long periods of time, the body breaks down and exhaustion occurs (Selye, 1984). I will assure you that after reading this book you will have learned many strategies in helping you to overcome your stress during your job search journey.

Chapter 16

Employment Stakeholders

"As president, I will bring all the parties and stakeholders together.
I am going to come up with a solution that respects the
environment and does not cause an upheaval in the economy"
Al Gore

It is amazing the number of people, groups, organizations, and agencies that impact our ability to find employment. This includes the smallest details, such as how a job specification is created to even the workspace that you will be working in. Besides managers and employees, there are also the shareholders, unions, customers, different national or local agencies, and local communities with major interests regarding decisions in the human resources field (Emanoil & Nicoleta, 2013). Stakeholders play a major role in the functioning of an organization.

A stakeholder is a person, group or organization that has interest or concern in an organization (BusinessDictionary.com, 2014). Essentially, a stakeholder is any person who is directly or indirectly affected by the functioning of a company. There are many, including internal and external stakeholders, involved in the employment process. Stakeholders may or may not be involved with the daily operations of the organization's functions. You might say, how can a stakeholder not be involved with what goes on in the organization's functions? We will look at several examples of a stakeholder's relationship with the organization within the coming sections.

Internal Stakeholders

Internal stakeholders are people who are already committed to serving the organization. These individuals or groups are directly involved and affected by its operations. The decisions and actions that these individuals make can immediately impact the image and repetition of the organization. The groups listed below all have a vested interest in its internal functions.

This does not mean that they do not have an impact or voice in the external situations or events.

Owners

Business owners overwhelmingly have a vested interest in all functions of the organization. Furthermore, business owners are directly involved in the day to day operations depending on the size of the organization. As the organization expands, the owner may delegate many of its functions to other trusted management personnel.

Executive management

Executive management personnel are usually those closest to the owner and are charged with ensuring that the organization is functioning according to its mission and vision. These managers are involved in the daily operations of the organization. Using a hotel establishment as an example, these individuals are generally directors of departments, such as human resources, marketing, food and beverage, housekeeping, and customer service. The goal is to make decisions that better the department.

Board members

Board members serve on the board of directors (BOD). Their role is to be a watch dog for the organization and to address potential internal and external threats. A BOD is a diverse group of board members that come from a number of venues, backgrounds and professions. These individuals may not be directly involved in the specific industry but have some type of stake in the success of the organization.

For example, a doctor might be a board member for a community center. This member might only be concerned with the implementation of health services to the community. Other board members might have expertise in a different area, but they all take pride in ensuring the project is a success.

Line staff

Non-management personnel have a vested interest in the organization for a number of reasons. One of the primary reasons for staff members being stakeholders is because this occupation is their chosen profession. School teachers and doctors are examples of individuals working in their targeted profession. Teachers take pride in educating students, while doctors take pride in healing patients.

When situations and events occur for individuals who have a vested interest in their job, they may be directly and indirectly involved in the functions of and changes in the industry, which might result in conflicts. A simple change in a curriculum or medical procedure are examples of such events that could affect stakeholders in their occupation.

Volunteers

Volunteers are those who donate their time to support an organization's cause. Volunteers are stakeholders because, like line staff members, they might share the same passion for providing services in a particular field or profession. The only difference between line staff and volunteers is that volunteers are not paid for their services, though they might perform the same tasks alongside a paid employee. Many parents volunteer at their children's schools while other individuals might work in homeless shelters or at a cancer treatment center, because they were directly affected by an event, prompting them to get personally involved in the cause.

While we would typically look at customers and stockholders as external stakeholders, these individuals can be internal stakeholders as well. Many employees are also customers of their place of employment and own shares of stock within their organizations. For example, I am sure that over 80% of all Wal-Mart employees also shop at their stores. Further, many organizations such as Staples and Hewlett Packard have stock options available for internal staff members.

External Stakeholders

External stakeholders, for the most part, are not involved in the internal functioning of the organization. However, these individuals can be affected by the organization's functions and they can affect how the organization functions. Examples of external stakeholders include:

Creditors

Creditors are entities, such as banks and other financial institutions, who provide funding to an organization to keep them functioning. These institutions are not directly or indirectly involved with an organization's functions. Their primary concern is if an organization can pay its debts. They are considered stakeholders, because as long as an organization progresses then banks will continue to lend to them, thereby profiting from the loans. However, these institutions are affected by situations that an organization might be engaged in. For example, if the business is being sued for a wrong doing, then a bank might elect to stop lending funds.

Suppliers

Suppliers are institutions, such as wholesale sellers of food and beverages to non-food related merchandise and materials, that provide an organization with products or services to help achieve its goals. A service in this case might be an accounting firm that maintains financial records. Vested interest is primarily concerned with reputation in such relationships. For example, if an organization has been charged with unethical business practices or supporting an underage smoking campaign, suppliers might terminate their relationship because of conflicts with values.

Government

There are many government entities that have a vested interest in organizations. These government entities are affected by the life cycle of an organization. Recall the chapter on an Organization's Life Cycle, which explains the different phases. Government agencies are involved in enforcing business laws and consumer protections. For example, our economy thrives off the success of businesses, therefore the government ensures that these businesses operate within the legal ramifications of the law. The government also has a vested in consumer rights. For example, the government might set a limit on how much sodium can be in a food product that a restaurant serves.

Stockholders

Stockholders are usually those who have purchased stocks with the intent of getting a return on their investments (ROI). This ROI is contingent on the success of the organization. Stockholders are not directly involved with the functions or daily operations. For example, many people with 401k plans have their money invested in stocks

It is important to learn who these stakeholders are, as well as their roles and responsibilities. This information becomes more imperative depending on the level of employment you are applying for. It may not be a necessity for an individual applying for a non-management position to fully have this knowledge. However, for an individual applying for any top level management position such as a public relations manager or a CEO, it would be imperative for these individuals to understand the roles and responsibilities of each party.

This chapter is also essential for job candidates who participate in panel interviews. If you understand the roles and responsibilities of the members on the panel, you can almost zoom in on why an individual asks a particular question or focuses on a specific function, and you can elaborate on that an issue.

Chapter 16. Exercise Explain your position as a stakeholder from the following viewpoints:

	Internal stakeholder	External stakeholder
Current place of employment		
Education institution		
Church		

References

Ahangar K., Rumaya J., Yaacob S.N., Abu Talib M (2013). Review on Marital Relationship among Iranian Immigrant. Applied Psychology. 4: 1-7.

Addams, L, Allred, A. T. (2013). The first step in proactively managing students' careers: Teaching self-SWOT analysis" academy of educational leadership journal. 17

Aicpa (2014). Educational requirements: 150 hours requirement for obtaining cpa certification. American institute of cpas. http://www.aicpa.org/BECOMEACPA/LICENSURE/REQUIREMENTS/Pages/default.aspx

Anomymous (2009). Microfoft corp; Microfoft surface expands availability to 12 Emea markets. Science letter. ISSN 15389111

Arora, N. (2013). Microsoft overcomes pc sales slide. Forbes. http://www.forbes.com/sites/nigamarora/2013/10/25/microsoft-overcomes-pc-sales-slide/

Asamoah, E. S., Chovancova, M., Alwis, C. D., Mudiynsela, S. Kumara, A., Guo, Y. (2011). Motivation for buying branded items: A cross country application of maslows hierarchy of needs in consumer decision making. Scientific papers of the university

of pardubice faculty of economics and administration. http://www.upce.cz/fes/veda-vyzkum/fakultni-casopisy/scipap/archiv/e-verze-sborniku/2011/sbornik-3-2011.pdf

Barlett, D. L. (2010). America: What went wrong? Google books. http://books.google.com/books?id=r0QLU3AWmIIC&pg=PA132&dq=eastern+airline+bankruptcy&hl=en&sa=X&ei=zB-iU6b-MIaT8QHKyYGoAQ&ved=0CBwQ6AEwAg#v=onepage&q=eastern%20airline%20bankruptcy&f=false

Bates, T. & Bradford, W. (2006b). *Traits and performance of minority venture-capital industry.* Retrieved from http://www.cofc.edu/~blocksonl/Minority%20Entrepreneurship/M

Beverly, T. (2010). Real-world intranets in 2010: SWOT analysis. Business information review. 27(2). DOI: 10.1177/0266382110370535

Bookey, B. S. (2006). The job interview. The Canadian nurse 102.3. Proquest.

Brenton, A. (2011). Overcoming the equal pay act and Title VII: Why federal sex-based employment discrimination laws should be replaced with a system for accrediting employers for their antidiscriminatory employment practices. (11)2. Wisconsin Journal of Law, Gender & Society

Bressler, M. S. (2014). Building the winning organization through high-impact hiring. Journal of management and marketing research.

Brown, S. and Huning, T. (2011). Intrinsic motivation and job satisfaction: The intervening role of goal orientation. Allied academies international conference

Browne, J. (2011). A reference for the best of us. Dating for dummies. Wiley publications. http://books.google.com/books?id=4EO01nVARG0C&printsec=frontcover&dq=Dating+is+a+form+of+courtship+consisting+of+social+activities+done+by+two+people+with+the+aim+of+each+assessing+the+other's+suitability+as+a+partner+in+an+intimate+relationship+or+as+a+spouse.+While+the+term+has+several+meanings,+it+usually+refers+to+the+act&hl=en&sa=X&ei=eiKcU-O6PIGVyASU 4HYDg&ved=0CBoQ-6AEwAQ#v=onepage&q&f=false

Business dictionary (2014b). Definition of management. http://www.businessdictionary.com/definition/leadership.html

Business dictionary (2014). Definition of stakeholder. http://www.businessdictionary.com/definition/stakeholder.html

Calo, T. J., Patterson, M. M., Decker, W. H. (2013). Employee perceptions of older workers' motivation in business, academia, and government (4)2. Journal of business and social science

Chantrill, C. (2014). U.S. education spending. US government spending. http://www.usgovernmentspending.com/us education spending 20.html

Coon, D. & Mitterer, J. O. (2010). Introduction to psychology: Gateways to mind and behavior with concept maps. *Belmont, CA: Wadsworth.*

Coldwell Banker (2014). Buyers market vs sellers market. http://cbplourde.com/buyers/buyers-market-vs-sellers-market/

Crossley, L., Media, D. (2014). *The advantages of a company doing internal & external hiring. Small business chron. http://smallbusiness.chron.com/ advantages-company-doing-internal-external-hiring-22017.html*

CSOSA (2013). *Types of prohibited discrimination. Court services and offender supervision agency for the district of Columbia. http://www. csosa.gov/about/employment/eeo/discrimination.aspx*

Cummings, T. and Vortey (2014). Theories of planned change. Ch 2-1. Organization development and change. Ebook. ISBN 1305143035, 9781305143036

Driscoll, E. (2011). It's all about who you know: Networking to get a job. Fox business. http://www.foxbusiness.com/personal-finance/2011/04/25/ know-networking-job/

Emanoil, M.; Nicoleta, M. S. (2013). Defining aspects of human resource management strategy within the general strategy of the modern organization. Annals of the university of Oradea, Economic science 22(1). Ebscohost

Ferry, N. M. (2006). Factors influencing career choices of adolescents and youth adults in rural Pennsylvania. Journal of extension.

Grensing-Pophal, L. (2012). The Everything Job Interview Book: All You Need to Stand Out in Today's Competitive Job Market. Adams Media. ISBN 1440531323, 9781440531323

Goodman, R. A. (2013). On the operationality of the Maslow need hierarchy. British journal of industrial relations.

Gupta, A. (2010). Organizational lifecycle and decline. Practical management. http://www.practical-management.com/Organization-Development/Organizational-lifecycle-and-decline.html

Hauenstein, P. (2010). Recruitment and selections. A project study on recruitment and selection in ims learning resources pvt. Ltd. http:// www.slideshare.net/harshalsk/recruitment-and-selection

Hoefer, M., Rytina, N., and Baker, B. C. (2010). Estimates of the unauthorized immigrant population residing in the United states: January 2009. Homeland security. Office of immigration statistics policy directorate. http://www.dhs.gov/xlibrary/assets/statistics/ publications/ois_ill_pe_2009.pdfhttp://www.dhs.gov/xlibrary/assets/ statistics/publications/ois_ill_pe_2009.pdf

Hussan, S. (2013). Apple profits decline despite iphone sales boost. BBC. Business. http://www.bbc.co.uk/news/business-24719728

International journal of entrepreneurial venturing (2013). Consolidation period in new ventures: how long does it take to establish a start-up. Inderscience publishers.

Jones, R. P., Cox, D., Navarro-Rivera, J., Dionne, E.J., and Galston, W. A. (2013). Citizenship, values, & cultural concerns: What Americans want from immigration reform. Public religion research institute.

Knezevich, A. (2012). Baltimore County sued again over alleged ADA violations. The Baltimore sun. http://articles.baltimoresun.com/2012-12-19/news/bs-md-co-ada-lawsuit-20121219_1_highway-worker-ada-violations-baltimore-county

Lachmann, S. (2013). Me before we: 8 reasons you're still single when you don't want to be. Psychology today.

Lazarus, R. S. (1966). Psychological stress and the coping process. New York:

McGraw-Hill.

Lemov, P. (2014). What it takes to win an age discrimination suit. Forbes.   http://www.forbes.com/sites/nextavenue/2013/04/30/what-it-takes-to-win-an-age-discrimination-suit/

Lowrey, Y (2007, April). A demographic review of minority business ownership. *Minorities in Business.* Retrieved from http://www.sba.gov/advo/research/rs298tot.pdf

Luxinnovation, (2008). Life cycle management = succession of stage of a product's life. The national agency for innovation and research in Luxembourg.

Mallin, M. L. and Finkle, T. A. (2011). Apple inc.: Product portfolio analysis. Journal of the international academy for case studies 17 (1).

McCabe, D. (2014). GOP rep. Kevin Cramer skeptical that lgbt workplace discrimination exists. Huffington post. http://www.huffingtonpost.com/2014/06/18/kevin-cramer-north-dakota_n_5507464.html

Manes, S. & Andrews, P. (1993). Gates; how Microsoft's mogul reinvented an industry- and made himself the richest man in America. ISBN:0671880748

Monroe, D. (2013). Untapped talent: Unleashing the power of the hidden workforce. http://books.google.com/books?id=guArJerJHtgC&pg=PA33&dq=leaving+work+to+culture+fit&hl=en&sa=X&ei=dKqUU9WoA9OKyATmkIH4AQ&ved=0CCIQ6AEwAg#v=onepage&q=leaving%20work%20to%20culture%20fit&f=false

Mosley, D., Mosley, D. Jr., Pietri P. (2014). Maslow's hierarchy of needs. Supervisory management. Google books.

Mudakavi, J. R. (2010). Magnitude and effects of air pollution. Principles snd practices of air pollutions control and analysis. Google books.

National Institute on Drug Abuse (2005). *Drug abuse is a major public health problem.* Retrieved from http://archives.drugabuse.gov/about/welcome/aboutdrugabuse/magnitude/

OPM (2014). Job analysis: Assessment and selection. U.S. Office of personal management. http://www.opm.gov/policy-data-oversight/assessment-and-selection/job-analysis/

O*net Online (2014). Online overview. http://www.onetonline.org/help/online/

Paquin, R. L. (2013). Blind dates and arranged marriages: Longitudinal processed of network orchestration. Organization studies 0170840612470230.

Pendrith, M. (2014). 12 reasons why new businesses fail. Believe by Mateusz M. http://www.evancarmichael.com/Starting-A-Business/866/12-REASONS-WHY-NEW-BUSINESSES-FAIL.html#cmtx_form

Phillips, J., and Gully, S. (2013). Selecting and hiring. Human resource management: Explore our new management. Pg (186). 1st editions. Cengage learning. ISBN: 1111533555, 9781111533557

Pope, M. (2012). Embracing and harnessing diversity in the US workforce: what have we learned? Int J Educ Vocat Guidance. DOI 10.1007/s10775-012-9215-x

Rangwala, S. (2012). Tips from the pros: How do I determine my worth? The Washington post. http://www.washingtonpost.com/jobs_articles/tips-from-the-pros/2012/10/09/f42ac2c4-117d-11e2-be82-c3411b7680a9_story.html

Ryan, M. (2014). 25 years since the Exxon Valdez oil spill – three things we remember. Research matters. http://www.researchmatters.

co/25-years-since-the-exxon-valdez-oil-spill-three-things-we-remember/

Sieczkowski, C. (2011). Steve Jobs and Bill Gates history: the dueling wizards. The international business times. http://www.ibtimes.com/steve-jobs-bill-gates-history-dueling-wizards-321739

Schwatz, N. D. (2013). Personal finance: In hiring, a friend in need is a prospect, indeed. The new york times. E:\career development\articles\In Hiring, a Friend in Need Is a Prospect, Indeed.htm

Selye, H. (1984). *The stress of life (2nd Ed.).* McGraw-Hill (2nd Edition).

Tsutsui, J. (2013). The transitional phase of mate selection in East Asian countries. International sociology. doi: 10.1177/0268580913484775

United States University, (2014). Personal branding. United States University website. http://www.usuniversity.edu/career-resources/personal-branding/

U.S. Department of education (2014). Annual publication of teacher shortage areas. U.S. Department of education. http://www2.ed.gov/about/offices/list/ope/pol/tsa.html

U.S. Department of housing and urban development (2014). About good neighbor next door. http://portal.hud.gov/hudportal/HUD?src=/program_offices/housing/sfh/reo/goodn/gnndabot

U.S. EEOC. (2013). Overview. U.S. Equal employment opportunity commission. http://www.eeoc.gov/eeoc/

U.S. EEOC (2) (2013). EEOC sues Battaglia distributing company for racial discrimination. U.S. Equal employment opportunity commission. http://www.eeoc.gov/eeoc/newsroom/release/8-14-13.cfm

U.S. EEOC (3) (2013). Religious discrimination. U.S. Equal employment opportunity commission. http://www.eeoc.gov/laws/types/religion.cfm

U.S. Legal Definition (2014). Job analysis law & legal definitions. http://definitions.uslegal.com/j/job-analysis/

U.S. Legal Definition(2) (2014). Job description law & legal definitions.. http://definitions.uslegal.com/j/job-description/

Williams, D. K. (2012). Dealing with a bad hire? The case to teach and adapt, rather than fire. Forbes Online. http://www.forbes.com/sites/davidkwilliams/2012/06/05/dealing-with-a-bad-hire-the-case-to-teach-and-adapt-rather-than-fire/

About the Author

Dr. Raymond Holmes is a Global Career Development Facilitator. He holds a doctorate degree in organizational leadership, and a Master of Management from the University of Phoenix. He also holds a Bachelor of Business Administration from the University of Baltimore.

Dr. Holmes has over 20 years of management and leadership experience in nonprofit, for-profit, and government organizations. He has a strong emphasis in training and development. He has over 14 years of teaching experience in workforce development and as a professor of business. The Doctor is a force to be reckoned with in his classes, using unorthodox teaching practices, a tough love approach, and thought provoking style. He engages, motivates and empowers individuals to be more productive once they return to their normal routine.

The Workforce Doctor

Printed in the United States
By Bookmasters